D1390720

AEROFILMS GUIDE

FOOTBALL
GROUNDS

✈ AEROFILMS GUIDE

FOOTBALL
GROUNDS

Edited by Dave Twydell

DIAL
PRESS

CONTENTS

Page 1: The old and the new. Millwall's new home is in the foreground while above the Den falls into disrepair.

Page 3: City rivals Liverpool (nearer) and Everton.

First published in 1993 by Dial Press
Second impression 1993

Dial Press is an imprint of Ian Allan Ltd, Terminal House, Station Approach, Shepperton, Surrey KT15 1HY

Aerial photography ©

 Aerofilms

Text © Ian Allan Ltd 1993
Football action photography © Empics
Photographs of Wembley reproduced by kind permission of Wembley plc

All rights reserved. No part of this publication may be reproduced, stored or transmitted in any form or by any means without prior written permission from the Publisher.

Printed by Ian Allan Printing Ltd
Coombelands House, Coombelands Lane, Addlestone, Weybridge, Surrey KT15 1HY

ISBN 0 7110 2157 0

Editor's Note

Every football fan knows that the game's grounds have changed greatly in recent years and are changing still more at the present time.

Government legislation concerning sports' ground safety and pressure from within the game for improved comforts for fans have combined to transform many old sites into new and improved stadia. All the grounds featured in this book were photographed during the 1992-3 season (when weather and air traffic control regulations permitted!) while this process of ground improvement was naturally going on. Building work in progress can thus be seen in some of the pictures. In some cases this work may have been completed after this book went to the printers and in other cases we show grounds as complete and intact where works will have subsequently begun. We will, of course, continue to update the coverage as fully as possible in future editions of this book. We have made every effort to ensure that all the information given in the entries for various clubs is accurate and complete but changes being made to grounds and other factors beyond the publisher's control may introduce errors for which the publishers can admit no consequential responsibility.

We would like to thank all the clubs who took the time and trouble to reply to our requests for information (which over 70 of the 92 did). We would also like to thank the Empics photo agency of Nottingham who supplied the football action pictures of each club which are also featured in this book.

WEMBLEY

Wembley Stadium, Wembley HA9 0DW

Telephone: 081-902 8833
Advance Tickets Tel No: 081-900 1234
Brief History: Inaugurated for F.A. Cup Final of 1923, venue for many major national and international matches including World Cup Final of 1966. Also used for major occasions in other sports and as venues for rock concerts and other entertainments.

(Total) Current Capacity: 80,000 (All seated)
Nearest Railway Station: Wembley Complex (BR), Wembley Central (BR & Tube), Wembley Park (tube)
Parking (Car): Limited parking at ground and nearby
Parking (Coach/Bus): As advised by police
Police Force: Metropolitan

ARSENAL

Arsenal Stadium, Avenell Road, Highbury, London, N5 1BU

Tel No: 071 226 0304
Advance Tickets Telephone: 071 359 0131
League: F.A. Premier
Brief History: Founded 1886 as Royal Arsenal, changed to Woolwich Arsenal in 1891, and Arsenal in 1914. Former grounds: Plumstead Common, Sportsman Ground, Manor Ground (twice), moved to Arsenal Stadium (Highbury) in 1913. Record attendance 73,295
(Total) Current Capacity: 41, 188 (18,140 Seated)

Club Colours: Red shirts with white sleeves, white shorts
Nearest Railway Station: Drayton Park & Finsbury Park. Arsenal (tube)
Parking (Car): Street Parking
Parking (Coach/Bus): Drayton park
Police Force and Tel No. Metropolitan (071 263 9090)
Disabled Visitors' Facilities
  Wheelchairs: Lower tier East Stand (few)
  Blind: Commentary available

KEY

C Club Offices
E Entrance(s) for visiting supporters

↑ North direction (approx)

❶ Avenell Road
❷ Highbury Hill
❸ Gillespie Road
❹ To Drayton Park BR Station (¼ mile)
❺ Arsenal Tube Station
❻ Clock End

Left: England International Paul Merson in the Gunners' early season clash with Sheffield Wednesday – the two teams were later to meet twice at Wembley.

ASTON VILLA

Villa Park, Trinity Road, Birmingham, B6 6HE

Tel No: 021 327 2299
Advance Tickets Telephone: 021 327 5353
League: F.A. Premier
Brief History: Founded in 1874. Founder Members Football League (1888). Former Grounds: Aston Park and Lower Aston Grounds & Perry Barr, moved to Villa Park (a development of the Lower Aston Grounds) in 1897. Record attendance 76,588
(Total) Current Capacity: 39,672 (20,462 Seated)
Visiting Supporters' Allocation: 4,510 (4,510 Seated)
Club Colours: Claret with blue sleeves shirts, white shorts

Nearest Railway Station: Witton
Parking (Car): Asda car park, Aston Hall Road
Parking (Coach/Bus): Asda car park, Aston Hall Road (special coach park for visiting supporters situated in Witton Lane).
Police Force and Tel No. West Midlands (021) 322 6010
Disabled Visitors' Facilities
  Wheelchairs: Trinity Road stand section
  Blind: Commentary by arrangement
Anticipated Development(s): Witton Lane stand being redeveloped for completion Autumn 1993.

KEY

C Club Offices
S Club Shop
E Entrance(s) for visiting supporters
R Refreshment bars for visiting supporters
T Toilets for visiting supporters

↑ North direction (approx)

❶ B4137 Witton Lane
❷ B4140 Witton Road
❸ Trinity Road
❹ A4040 Aston Lane to A34 Walsall Road
❺ To Aston Expressway & M6
❻ Holte End
❼ Visitors' Car Park

Left: In the doldrums at Anfield, then regularly on the scoresheet for Villa – Dean Saunders in a characteristic pose.

BARNET

Underhill Stadium, Barnet Lane, Barnet, Herts, EN5 2BE

Tel No: 081 441 6932
Advance Tickets Tel No: 081 449 4173
League: 2nd Division
Brief History: Founded 1888 as Barnet Alston. Changed name to Barnet (1919). Former grounds: Queens Road & Totteridge Lane. Promoted to Football League 1991. Record attendance 11,026.
(Total) Current Capacity: 6,009 (1,000 Seated)
Visiting Supporters' Allocation: 1,250 (None Seated)

Club Colours: Amber shirts, black shorts.
Nearest Railway Station: New Barnet (High Barnet - Tube)
Parking (Car): Street Parking & High Barnet Station
Parking (Coach/Bus): As directed by Police
Police Force and Tel No: Metropolitan (081) 200 2212
Disabled Visitors' Facilities
  Wheelchairs: Barnet Lane (Social Club end - few spaces)
  Blind: No special facility

KEY

C Club Offices
S Club Shop
E Entrance(s) for visiting supporters
R Refreshment bars for visiting supporters
T Toilets for visiting supporters

⬆ North direction (approx)

❶ Barnet Lane
❷ Westcombe Drive
❸ A1000 Barnet Hill
❹ New Barnet BR Station (1 mile)
❺ To High Barnet Tube Station, M1 & M25

Left: Prolific striker Gary Bull in the familiar Bees' colours, a leading figure in the Club's 1993 promotion to the 2nd Division.

BARNSLEY

Oakwell Ground, Grove Street, Barnsley, S71 1ET

Tel No: 0226 295353
Advance Tickets Tel No: 0226 295353
League: 1st Division
Brief History: Founded 1887 as Barnsley St Peter's, changed name to Barnsley in 1897. Former Ground: Doncaster Road, Worsboro Bridge until 1888. Record attendance 40,255.
(Total) Current Capacity: 26,586 (2,154 Seated)
Club Colours: Red shirts, white shorts

Nearest Railway Station: Barnsley Exchange
Parking (Car): Queen's Ground car park
Parking (Coach/Bus): Queen's Ground car park
Police Force and Tel No: South Yorkshire (0226) 206161
Disabled Visitors' Facilities
   Wheelchairs: Disabled stand (Main Stand)
   Blind: Commentary available

KEY

C Club Offices
S Club Shop
E Entrance(s) for visiting supporters
R Refreshment bars for visiting supporters
T Toilets for visiting supporters

↑ North direction (approx)

❶ A628 Pontefract Road
❷ A61
❸ To Barnsley Exchange BR Station & M1 Junction 37 (2 miles)
❹ Queen's Ground Car Park
❺ Spion Kop
❻ (New) Brewery Stand

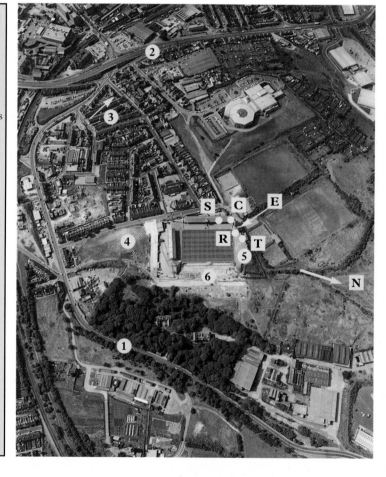

Right: Red-shirted John Pearson leaps for the ball, together with Stephen Howey of Newcastle.

BIRMINGHAM CITY

St Andrew's, St. Andrew's Street, Birmingham, B9 4NH

Tel No: 021 772 0101
Advance Tickets Tel No: 021 772 0101
League: 1st Division
Brief History: Founded 1875, as Small Heath Alliance. Changed to Small Heath in 1888, Birmingham in 1905, Birmingham City in 1945. Former Grounds: Arthur Street, Ladypool Road, Muntz Street, moved to St. Andrew's in 1906. Record attendance 68,844.
(Total) Current Capacity: 27,545 (8,395 Seated)
Visiting Supporters' Allocation: 5,700 (808 Seated)

Club Colours: Blue & white shirts, white shorts
Nearest Railway Station: Birmingham New Street
Parking (Car): Street parking, plus Coventry Road & Cattell Road car parks
Parking (Coach/Bus): Tilton Road
Police Force and Tel No: West Midlands (021) 772 1169
Disabled Visitors' Facilities
　Wheelchairs: Remploy stand (St. Andrew's Street), advanced notice required.
　Blind: No special facilities.

KEY

C Club Offices
S Club Shop
E Entrance(s) for visiting supporters
R Refreshment bars for visiting supporters
T Toilets for visiting supporters

↑ North direction (approx)

❶ Car Park
❷ B4128 Cattell Road
❸ Tilton Road
❹ Garrison Lane
❺ To A4540 & A38 (M)
❻ To City Centre and New Street BR Station (1½ miles)

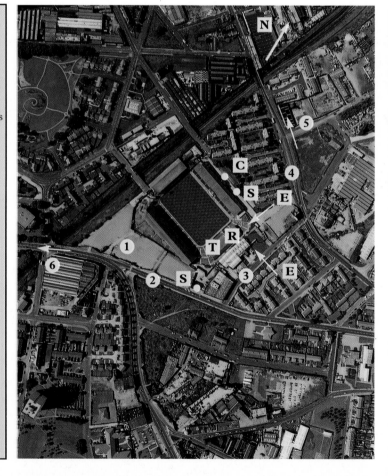

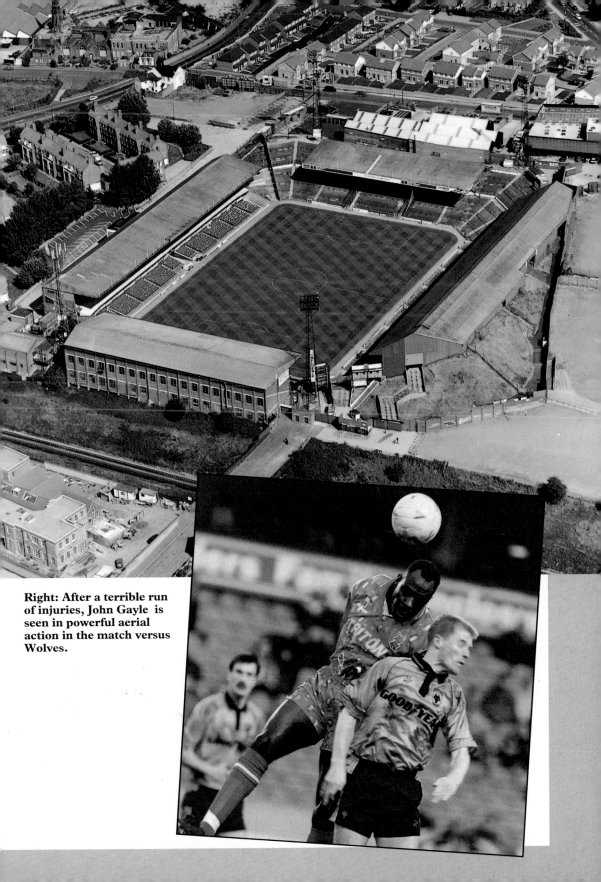

Right: After a terrible run of injuries, John Gayle is seen in powerful aerial action in the match versus Wolves.

BLACKBURN ROVERS

Ewood Park, Blackburn, Lancashire, BB2 4JF

Telephone: 0254 55432
Advance Tickets Tel No: 0254 55432 (696767 Credit card line)
League: F.A. Premier
Brief History: Founded 1875. Former Grounds: Oozebooth, Pleasington Cricket Ground, Alexandra Meadows. Moved to Ewood Park in 1890. Founder members of Football League (1888). Record attendance 61,783.
(Total) Current Capacity: 20,337 (7,657 Seated)
Visiting Supporters' Allocation: 4,800 (None Seated)
Club Colours: Blue & white halved shirts, white shorts

Nearest Railway Station: Blackburn Central
Parking (Car): Street parking
Parking (Coach/Bus): As directed by Police
Police Force and Tel No: Lancashire (0254 51212)
Disabled Visitors' Facilities
  Wheelchairs :Walkersteel Stand (Riverside Lane) - few
  Blind: Commentary available
Anticipated Development(s): All-seater stadium completion in 1994, with approx 30,000 seats.

KEY

C Club Offices
E Entrance(s) for visiting supporters

⬆ North direction (approx)

❶ A666 Great Bolton Street
❷ Nuttall Street
❸ Kidder Street
❹ Town Centre & Blackburn Central BR Station (1½ miles)
❺ To Darwen and Bolton

Left: A familiar sight at Ewood Park as Alan Shearer heads towards the goal, and Rovers win again.

BLACKPOOL

Bloomfield Road, Blackpool, Lancashire, FY1 6JJ

Telephone: 0253 404331
Advance Tickets Tel No: 0253 404331
League: 2nd Division
Brief History: Founded 1887, merged with 'South Shore' (1899). Former grounds: Raikes Hall (twice) and Athletic Grounds, Stanley Park. South Shore played at Cow Cap Lane, moved to Bloomfield Road in 1899. Record attendance 38,098
(Total) Current Capacity: 10,337 (2,987 Seated)
Visiting Supporters' Allocation: 2,500 min.(None Seated)
Club Colours: Tangerine shirts, white shorts

Nearest Railway Station: Blackpool South
Parking (Car): At Ground & street parking (also behind West Stand - from M55)
Parking (Coach/Bus): Mecca car park (behind East End,
(also behind West Stand - from M55)
Police Force and Tel No: Lancashire (0253 293933)
Disabled Visitors' Facilities
  Wheelchairs: By players entrance
  Blind: Commentary available
Anticipated Development(s): Plans for new ground/complex in same area anticipated for 1994/5 season.

KEY
C Club Offices
E Entrance(s) for visiting supporters

↑ North direction (approx)

❶ Car Parks
❷ To Blackpool South BR Station (1/2 mile) and M55 Junction 4
❸ Bloomfield Drive
❹ Central Drive
❺ Henry Street
❻ Blackpool Rugby & Greyhound Stadium
❼ Blackpool Tower

Left: Experienced forward Dave Bamber, formerly a Swindon Town favourite, but now in the tangerine of Blackpool.

BOLTON WANDERERS

Burnden Park, Manchester Road, Bolton, BL3 2QR

Telephone: 0204 389200
Advance Tickets Tel No: 0204 21101
League: 1st Division
Brief History: Founded 1874 as Christ Church until 1877. Former Grounds: several very basic fields were used before move to Pikes Lane in 1880, moved to Burnden Park in 1895. Founder-members of Football League (1888). Record attendance 69,912.
(Total) Current Capacity: 22,772 (8,000 Seated)

Club Colours: White shirts, blue shorts
Nearest Railway Station: Bolton Trinity Street
Parking (Car): Rosehill car park, Manchester Road
Parking (Coach/Bus): Rosehill car park, Manchester Road
Police Force and Tel No: Greater Manchester (0204 22466)
Disabled Visitors' Facilities
    Wheelchairs: Manchester Road (few)
    Blind: No special facility

KEY

E Entrance(s) for visiting supporters

R Refreshment bars for visiting supporters

T Toilets for visiting supporters

↑ North direction (approx)

❶ Car Parks
❷ B6536 Manchester Road
❸ A666 St Peter's Way
❹ Bolton Trinity Street BR Station (1/2 mile)
❺ To M61 Junction 3 (3 miles)
❻ Supermarket

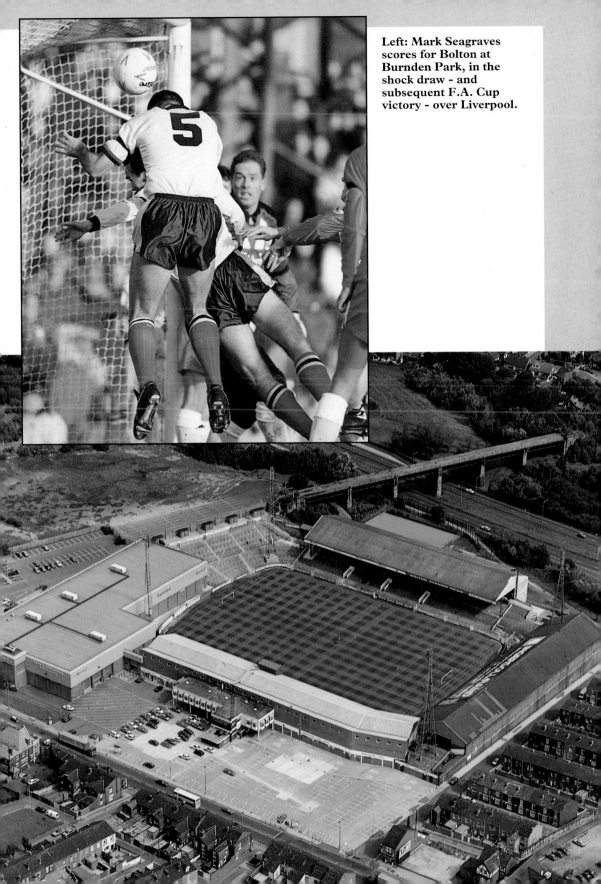

Left: Mark Seagraves scores for Bolton at Burnden Park, in the shock draw - and subsequent F.A. Cup victory - over Liverpool.

A.F.C. BOURNEMOUTH

Dean Court, Bournemouth, Dorset BH7 7AF

Telephone: 0202 395381
Advance Tickets Tel No: 0202 395381
League: 2nd Division
Brief History: Founded 1890 as Boscombe St. John's, changed to Boscombe (1899), Bournemouth & Boscombe Athletic (1923) and A.F.C. Bournemouth (1971). Former grounds: Kings Park (twice) and Castlemain Road, Pokesdown. Moved to Dean Court in 1910. Record attendance 28,799.
(Total) Current Capacity: 10,750 (3,131 Seated)
Visiting Supporters' Allocation: 2,060 (190 Seated)

Club Colours: Red with white 'V' shirts, black with white piping shorts.
Nearest Railway Station: Bournemouth
Parking (Car): Large car park adjacent ground
Parking (Coach/Bus): Large car park adjacent ground
Police Force and Tel No: Dorset (0202) 552099
Disabled Visitors' Facilities
  Wheelchairs: South Stand (prior arrangement)
  Blind: No special facility

KEY

C Club Offices
S Club Shop
E Entrance(s) for visiting supporters
R Refreshment bars for visiting supporters
T Toilets for visiting supporters

↑ North direction (approx)

❶ Car Park
❷ A338 Wessex Way
❸ To Bournemouth BR Station (1½ miles)
❹ To A31 & M27

Right: Seen here wearing the Cherries' change strip, Efaw Ekoko was a target for several Premier League sides before his move to Norwich.

BRADFORD CITY

Valley Parade, Bradford, BD8 7DY

Tel No: 0274 306062
Advance Tickets Tel No: 0274 307050
League: 2nd Division
Brief History: Founded 1903 (formerly Manningham Northern Union Rugby Club founded in 1876). Continued use of Valley Parade, joined 2nd Division on re-formation. Record attendance 39,146.
(Total) Current Capacity: 14,810 (6,500 Seated)
Club Colours: Claret & amber shirts, claret shorts

Nearest Railway Station: Bradford Forster Square

Parking (Car): Street parking and car parks

Parking (Coach/Bus): As directed by Police

Police Force and Tel No: West Yorkshire (0274 723422)

Disabled Visitors' Facilities
  Wheelchairs: N & P Stand
  Blind: No special facility

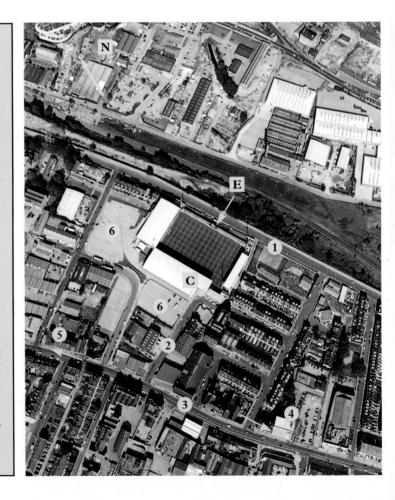

KEY

C Club Offices
E Entrance(s) for visiting supporters

↑ North direction (approx)

❶ Midland Road
❷ Valley Parade
❸ A650 Manningham Lane
❹ To City Centre, Forster Square and Interchange BR Stations M606 &M62
❺ To Keighley
❻ Car Parks

Right: Brian Tinnion in typical forceful action for City in a Division 2 game at Valley Parade.

27

BRENTFORD

Griffin Park, Braemar Road, Brentford, Middlesex, TW8 0NT

Tel No: 081 847 2511
Advance Tickets Tel No: 081 847 2511
League: 2nd Division
Brief History: Founded 1889. Former Grounds: Clifden House Ground, Benn's Field (Little Ealing), Shotters Field, Cross Roads, Boston Park Cricket Ground, moved to Griffin Park in 1904. Founder-members Third Division (1920). Record attendance 39,626.
(Total) Current Capacity: 12,452 (4,000 Seated)

Club Colours: Red & white striped shirts, black shorts
Nearest Railway Station: Brentford Central, South Ealing (tube)
Parking (Car): Street parking (restricted)
Parking (Coach/Bus): Layton Road car park
Police Force and Tel No: Metropolitan (081 569 9728)
Disabled Visitors' Facilities
   Wheelchairs: Braemar Road
   Blind: Commentary available

KEY
- **C** Club Offices
- **S** Club Shop
- **E** Entrance(s) for visiting supporters
- **R** Refreshment bars for visiting supporters
- **T** Toilets for visiting supporters

↑ North direction (approx)

❶ Ealing Road
❷ Braemar Road
❸ Brook Road South
❹ To M4 (¼ mile) & South Ealing Tube Station (1 mile)
❺ Brentford Central BR Station
❻ To A315 High Street & Kew Bridge

Left: Bees' favourite Gary Blissett, one of the country's leading goalscorers, who came from Crewe Alexandra.

BRIGHTON & HOVE ALBION

Goldstone Ground, Newtown Road, Hove, Sussex, BN3 7DE

Tel No: 0273 739535
Advance Tickets Tel No: 0273 778855
League: 2nd Division
Brief History: Founded 1900 as Brighton and Hove Rangers, changed to Brighton and Hove Albion in 1901. Former Grounds: Home Farm (Withdean) and County Ground, moved to Goldstone Ground in 1902. Founder members Third Division (1920). Record attendance 36,747.
(Total) Current Capacity: 17,607 (5,274 Seated)
Visiting Supporters' Allocation: 3,078 (738 Seated)

Club Colours: Blue & white striped shirts, and matching shorts
Nearest Railway Station: Hove
Parking (Car): Greyhound Stadium and street parking
Parking (Coach/Bus): Conway Street
Police Force and Tel No: Sussex (0273 778922)
Disabled Visitors' Facilities
  Wheelchairs: Newtown Road (South West corner)
  Blind: Commentary available

KEY

C Club Offices
S Club Shop
E Entrance(s) for visiting supporters
R Refreshment bars for visiting supporters
T Toilets for visiting supporters

↑ North direction (approx)

❶ A27 Old Shoreham Road
❷ Nevill Road
❸ To A2038 & A23
❹ Goldstone Lane
❺ Newtown Road
❻ Greyhound Stadium
❼ Hove BR Station

Left: Matthew Edwards is seen in full flight during a Seagulls Coca Cola League Cup match.

BRISTOL CITY

Ashton Gate, Winterstoke Road, Ashton Road, Bristol, BS3 2EJ

Tel No: 0272 632812
Advance Tickets Tel No: 0272 632812
League: 1st Division
Brief History: Founded 1894 as Bristol South End changed to Bristol City in 1897. Former Ground: St. John's Lane, Bedminster, moved to Ashton Gate in 1904. Record attendance 43,335
(Total) Current Capacity: 25,271 (16,000 Seated)
Club Colours: Red shirts, white shorts

Nearest Railway Station: Bristol Temple Meads
Parking (Car): Street parking
Parking (Coach/Bus): Marsh Road
Police Force and Tel No: Avon/Somerset (0272 277777)
Disabled Visitors' Facilities
  Wheelchairs: Advanced notice required
  Blind: Commentary available
Anticipated Development(s): New stand at open end 1994.

KEY
C Club Offices
S Club Shop
E Entrance(s) for visiting supporters
R Refreshment bars for visiting supporters
T Toilets for visiting supporters

⬆ North direction (approx)

❶ A370 Ashton Road
❷ A3209 Winterstoke Road
❸ To Temple Meads Station (1½ miles)
❹ To City Centre, A4, M32 & M4
❺ Clifton Suspension Bridge
❻ River Avon

Left: In the match versus Derby County, City's Micky Mellon fights for the ball - and for Marco Gabbiadini's shirt.

BRISTOL ROVERS

Twerton Park, Bath, Avon

(Office: 199 Two Mile Hill Road, Kingswood, Bristol, BS15 7AZ)

Tel No: 0272 352508

Advance Tickets Tel No: 0272 352508

League: 2nd Division

Brief History: Founded 1883 as Black Arabs, changed to Eastville Rovers (1884), Bristol Eastville Rovers (1896) and Bristol Rovers in 1897. Former Grounds: Purdown, Three Acres, The Downs (Horfield), Ridgeway, Bristol Stadium (Eastville) moved to Twerton Park in 1986. Record attendance (at Eastville) 38,472. (At Twerton Park) 9,813.

(Total) Current Capacity: 8,800 (1,006 Seated)

Visiting Supporters' Allocation: 1,125 (None Seated)

Club Colours: Blue & white quartered shirts, white shorts

Nearest Railway Station: Bath Spa

Parking (Car): Street parking (limited) Western Island, Lower Bristol Road

Parking (Coach/Bus): Avon Street

Police Force and Tel No: Avon/Somerset (0225 444343)

Disabled Visitors' Facilities
  Wheelchairs: Family stand
  Blind: Commentary available by arrangement

Anticipated Development(s): Relocation to New Stadium - 1995/6 season at Severnside, Bristol

---

KEY

E Entrance(s) for visiting supporters

R Refreshment bars for visiting supporters

T Toilets for visiting supporters

↑ North direction (approx)

❶ High Street (Twerton)
❷ A36 Lower Bristol Road
❸ (Bath) City Centre & Bath Spa BR Station (1½ miles)
❹ To Bristol
❺ River Avon

Left: Not a regular in the Rovers' side, John Taylor celebrates a goal at Twerton Park.

BURNLEY

Turf Moor, Brunshaw Road, Burnley, Lancs, BB10 4BX

Tel No: 0282 27777
Advance Tickets Tel No: 0282 27777
League: 2nd Division
Brief History: Founded 1882, Burnley Rovers (Rugby Club) combined with another Rugby Club, changed to soccer and name to Burnley. Moved from Calder Vale to Turf Moor in 1882. Founder-members Football League (1888). Record attendance 54,775.
(Total) Current Capacity: 20,912 (7,437 Seated)
Club Colours: Claret with blue sleeved shirts, white shorts

Nearest Railway Station: Burnley Central

Parking (Car): Church Street and Fulledge Rec. (car parks)

Parking (Coach/Bus): As directed by Police

Police Force and Tel No: Lancashire (0282 25001)

Disabled Visitors' Facilities
  Wheelchairs: Bob Lord (Brunshaw Road) Stand (few)
  Blind: No special facility

KEY
C Club Offices
E Entrance(s) for visiting supporters

↑ North direction (approx)

❶ Brunshaw Road
❷ Belvedere Road
❸ Burnley Central BR Station (½ mile)
❹ Cricket Ground

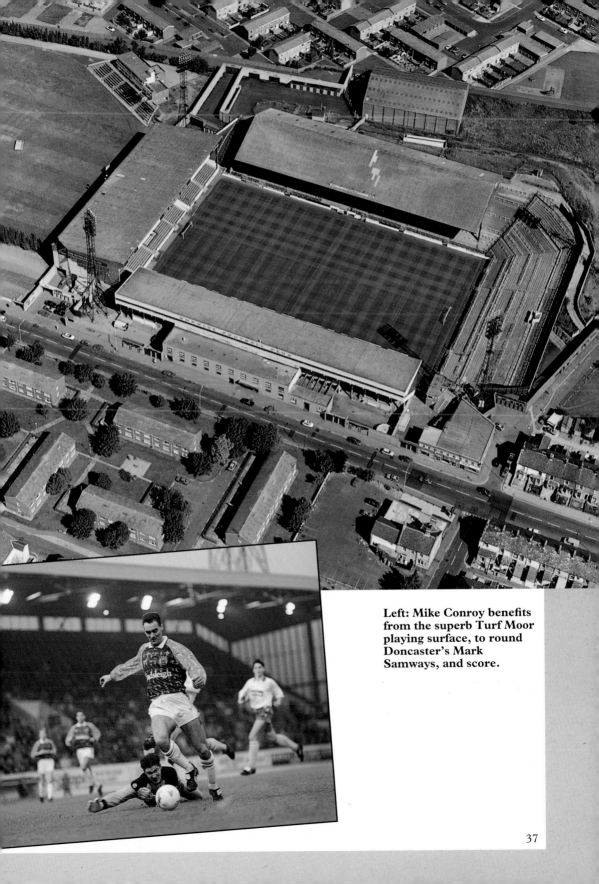

Left: Mike Conroy benefits from the superb Turf Moor playing surface, to round Doncaster's Mark Samways, and score.

BURY

Gigg Lane, Bury, Lancashire, BL9 9HR

Tel No: 061 764 4881
Advance Tickets Tel No: 061 764 4881
League: 3rd Division
Brief History: Founded 1885, no former names or former grounds. Record attendance 35,000
(Total) Current Capacity: 12,900 (Currently 2,500 anticipated 6,900 Seated)
Club Colours: White shirts, navy shorts
Nearest Railway Station: Bury Interchange
Parking (Car): Street parking

Parking (Coach/Bus): As directed by Police
Police Force and Tel No: Greater Manchester (061 872 5050)
Disabled Visitors' Facilities
  Wheelchairs: Corner South Stand/Cemetery Road
  Blind: Radio commentary (Press box)
Anticipated Development(s): Rebuilt South Stand completion Jan 1994.

KEY

C Club Offices
S Club Shop
E Entrance(s) for visiting supporters
R Refreshment bars for visiting supporters
T Toilets for visiting supporters

⬆ North direction (approx)

❶ Car Park
❷ Gigg Lane
❸ A56 Manchester Road
❹ Town Centre & Bury Interchange (Metrolink) (3/4 mile)

Left: Shaker's David Adekola slots the ball home in the match versus Carlisle United at Gigg Lane.

CAMBRIDGE UNITED

Abbey Stadium, Newmarket Road, Cambridge, CB5 8LL

Telephone: 0223 241237
Advance Tickets Tel No: 0223 241237
League: 2nd Division
Brief History: Founded 1913 as Abbey United, changed to Cambridge United in 1949. Former Grounds: Midsummer Common, Stourbridge Common, Station Farm Barnwell (The Celery Trenches) & Parker's Piece, moved to Abbey Stadium in 1933. Record attendance 14,000.
(Total) Current Capacity: 10,100 (3,410 Seated)

Visiting Supporters' Allocation: 2,266 (366 Seated)
Club Colours: Amber shirts, black shorts
Nearest Railway Station: Cambridge (2 miles)
Parking (Car): Coldhams Common
Parking (Coach/Bus): Coldhams Common
Police Force and Tel No: Cambridge (0223 358966)
Disabled Visitors' Facilities
　Wheelchairs: 12 spaces
　Blind: No special facility

KEY

C Club Offices
S Club Shop
E Entrance(s) for visiting supporters
R Refreshment bars for visiting supporters
T Toilets for visiting supporters

↑ North direction (approx)

❶ A1134 Newmarket Road
❷ To A11 & Newmarket
❸ To City Centre, Cambridge BR Station (2 miles) & M11
❹ Whitehill Road

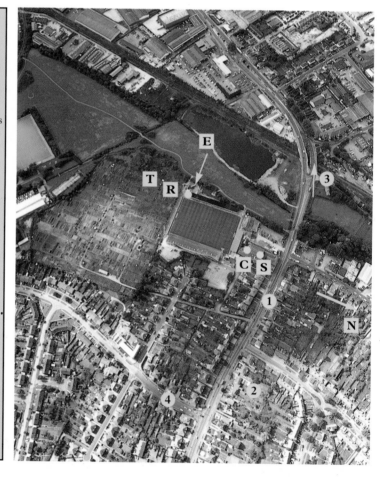

Left: Steve Claridge (in amber shirt) races for the ball, together with Andy Awford of Portsmouth.

CARDIFF CITY

Ninian Park, Sloper Road, Cardiff, CF1 8SX

Tel No: 0222 398636
Advance Tickets Tel No: 0222 398636
League: 2nd Division
Brief History: Founded 1899. Former Grounds: Riverside Cricket Club, Roath, Sophia Gardens, Cardiff Arms Park & The Harlequins Rugby Ground, moved to Ninian Park in 1910. Ground record attendance 61,566 (Wales v. England, 1961)
(Total) Current Capacity: 21,403 (5,563 Seated)
Club Colours: Blue shirts, blue shorts

Nearest Railway Station: Cardiff Central
Parking (Car): Sloper Road & street parking
Parking (Coach/Bus): Sloper Road
Police Force and Tel No: South Wales (0222 222111)
Disabled Visitors' Facilities
  Wheelchairs: Corner Canton Stand/Popular Bank
  Blind: No special facility
Anticipated Development(s): Eventual all seating stadium.

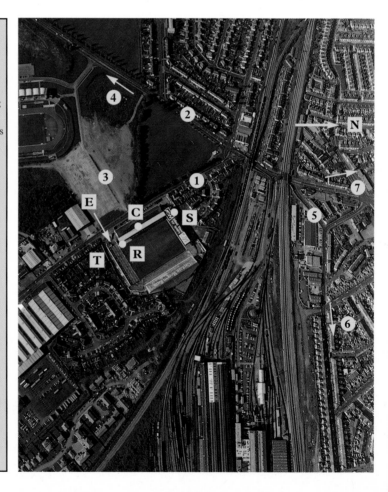

KEY

C Club Offices
S Club Shop
E Entrance(s) for visiting supporters
R Refreshment bars for visiting supporters
T Toilets for visiting supporters

↑ North direction (approx)

❶ Sloper Road
❷ B4267 Leckwith Road
❸ Car Park
❹ To A4232 & M4 Junction 33 (8 miles)
❺ Ninian Park Road
❻ To City Centre & Cardiff Central BR Station (1 mile)
❼ To A48 Western Avenue, A48M, and M4 Junctions 32 and 29

Left: Damon Searle, who became a regular player in the Cardiff squad during the 1990/91 season.

CARLISLE UNITED

Brunton Park, Warwick Road, Carlisle, CA1 1LL

Tel No: 0228 26237
Advance Tickets Tel No: 0228 26237
League: 3rd Division
Brief History: Founded 1904 as Carlisle United (previously named Shaddongate United). Former Grounds: Millholme Bank and Devonshire Park, moved to Brunton Park in 1909. Record attendance 27,500.
(Total) Current Capacity: 18,506 (2,162 Seated)
Club Colours: Royal blue shirts, white shorts

Nearest Railway Station: Carlisle Citadel
Parking (Car): Rear of ground
Parking (Coach/Bus): St. Aiden's Road car park
Police Force and Tel No: Cumbria (0228 28191)
Disabled Visitors' Facilities
  Wheelchairs: Front of Main Stand (prior arrangement)
  Blind: Commentary available

KEY

C Club Offices
E Entrance(s) for visiting supporters
R Refreshment bars for visiting supporters
T Toilets for visiting supporters

↑ North direction (approx)

❶ A69 Warwick Road
❷ M6 Junction 43
❸ Carlisle Citadel BR Station (1 mile)
❹ Greystone Road
❺ Car Park

Left: United's Paul Proudlock (on the right) in action at Gigg Lane, with Bury's Tony Rigby.

CHARLTON ATHLETIC

The Valley, Floyd Road, Charlton, London, SE7 8BL

Tel No: 081 293 4567
Advance Tickets Tel No: 081 293 4567
League: 1st Division
Brief History: Founded 1905. Former grounds: Siemens Meadows, Woolwich Common, Pound Park, Angerstein Athletic Ground, The Mount Catford, Selhurst Park (Crystal Palace FC), Boleyn Ground (West Ham United FC), The Valley (1919-1923, 1924-85, 1992-). Founder Members 3rd Division South. Record attendance 75,031.

(Total) Current Capacity: 12,000 (9,000 Seated)
Club Colours: Red shirts, white shorts
Nearest Railway Station: Charlton
Parking (Car): Street parking
Parking (Coach/Bus): As directed by Police
Police Force and Tel No: Metropolitan (081 853 8212)
Disabled Visitors' Facilities
  Wheelchairs: East Stand
  Blind: No special facility

KEY
C Club Offices
E Entrance(s) for visiting supporters

↑ North direction (approx)

❶ Harvey Gardens
❷ A206 Woolwich Road
❸ Valley Grove
❹ Floyd Road
❺ Charlton BR Station
❻ River Thames
❼ Thames Barrier

Left: Back at the Valley at last, and Charlton's Peter Garland in action in the F.A. Cup game with Leeds United.

CHELSEA

Stamford Bridge, Fulham Road, London, SW6 1HS

Tel No: 071 385 5545
Advance Tickets Tel No: 071 385 5545
League: F.A. Premier
Brief History: Founded 1905. Admitted to Football League (2nd Division) on formation. Stamford Bridge venue for F.A. Cup Finals 1919-1922. Record attendance 82,905.
(Total) Current Capacity: 36,000 (19,800 Seated)
Club Colours: Blue shirts, blue shorts
Nearest Railway Station: Fulham Broadway

Parking (Car): Street parking
Parking (Coach/Bus): As directed by Police
Police Force and Tel No: Metropolitan (071 385 1212)
Disabled Visitors' Facilities
  Wheelchairs: East Stand
  Blind: No special facility
Anticipated Development(s): North Stand conversion to 2 tier all seater stand (with part of terrace remaining), construction during 1993/94 season.

KEY

C Club Offices
S Club Shop
E Entrance(s) for visiting supporters
R Refreshment bars for visiting supporters
T Toilets for visiting supporters

↑ North direction (approx)

❶ A308 Fulham Road
❷ Central London
❸ Fulham Broadway Tube Station
❹ South (Shed) Terrace

Left: Graham Stuart leads the chase for the ball, alongside Simon Rodger of Crystal Palace.

CHESTER CITY

The Deva Stadium, Bumpers Lane, Chester

Tel No: 0244 371376
Advance Tickets Tel No: 0244 373829
League: 3rd Division
Brief History: Founded 1884 from amalgamation of Chester Wanderers and Chester Rovers. Former Grounds: Faulkner Street, Lightfoot Street, Whipcord Lane, Sealand Road, Moss Rose (Macclesfield Town F.C.), moved to Deva Stadium in 1992. Record attendance (Sealand Road) 20,500.
(Total) Current Capacity: 6,000 (3,284 Seated)

Visiting Supporters' Allocation: 2,438 max.(Seated 1,238 max.)
Club Colours: Blue shirts, white shorts
Nearest Railway Station: Chester (1 1/2 miles)
Parking (Car): Car park at ground
Parking (Coach/Bus): Car park at ground
Police Force and Tel No: Cheshire (0244 350222)
Disabled Visitors' Facilities
  Wheelchairs: West and East Stand
  Blind: Facility available

KEY
C Club Offices
S Club Shop
E Entrance(s) for visiting supporters
R Refreshment bars for visiting supporters
T Toilets for visiting supporters

↑ North direction (approx)

❶ Bumpers Lane
❷ To City Centre and Chester BR Station (1 1/2 miles)
❸ Car Park

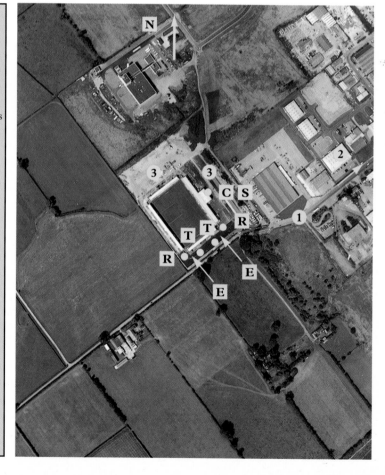

50

Left: Chester 'keeper Billy Stewart gets to the ball first, with Hull City's Russ Wilcox close by.

CHESTERFIELD

Recreation Ground, Saltergate, Chesterfield, S40 4SX

Tel No: 0246 209765
Advance Tickets Tel No: 0246 209765
League: 3rd Division
Brief History: Founded 1866. Former Ground: Spital Vale. Formerly named Chesterfield Town. Record attendance 30,968
(Total) Current Capacity: 11,308 (2,608 Seated)
Club Colours: Blue and white striped shirts, white shorts

Nearest Railway Station: Chesterfield
Parking (Car): Saltergate car park, street parking
Parking (Coach/Bus): As directed by Police
Police Force and Tel No: Derbyshire (0246 220100)
Disabled Visitors' Facilities
   Wheelchairs: Saltergate Stand
   Blind: No special facility

KEY

C Club Offices

S Club Shop

E Entrance(s) for visiting supporters

R Refreshment bars for visiting supporters

T Toilets for visiting supporters

↑ North direction (approx)

❶ Saltergate
❷ Cross Street
❸ St Margaret's Drive
❹ A632 West Bars
❺ To A617 & M1 Junction 29

Left: Trevor Hebberd beats Liverpool goalkeeper Bruce Grobbelaar, to score in the Coca Cola League Cup clash.

COLCHESTER UNITED

Layer Road Ground, Colchester, CO2 7JJ

Tel No: 0206 574042
Advance Tickets Tel No: 0206 574042
League: 3rd Division
Brief History: Founded 1937, joined Football League 1950, relegated 1990, promoted 1992. Record attendance 19,072.
(Total) Current Capacity: 7,223 (1,169 Seated)
Club Colours: Royal Blue & White shirts, Royal Blue shorts

Nearest Railway Station: Colchester North
Parking (Car): Street parking
Parking (Coach/Bus): Boadicea Way
Police Force and Tel No: Essex (0206 762212)
Disabled Visitors' Facilities
  Wheelchairs: Main Stand (limited)
  Blind: Commentary available (booking necessary)

KEY

C Club Offices
S Club Shop
E Entrance(s) for visiting supporters
R Refreshment bars for visiting supporters
T Toilets for visiting supporters

↑ North direction (approx)

❶ B1026 Layer Road
❷ Town Centre & Colchester North BR Station (2 miles)
❸ Main Stand
❹ Popular Side

Left: Tony English in action for United, in the Club's first season back in the Football League.

COVENTRY CITY

Highfield Stadium, King Richard Street, Coventry CV2 4FW.

Tel No: 0203 223535
Advance Tickets Tel No: 0203 225545
League: F.A. Premier
Brief History: Founded 1883 as Singers F.C., changed name to Coventry City in 1898. Former grounds; Dowell's Field, Stoke Road Ground, moved to Highfield Road in 1899. Record attendance, 51,455.
(Total) Current Capacity: 25,311 (17,650 Seated)
Visiting Supporters' Allocation: 4,916 (2,766 Seated)
Club Colours: Sky blue, navy and white shirts, sky blue & white shorts.

Nearest Railway Station: Coventry.
Parking (Car): Street parking
Parking (Coach/Bus): Gosford Green Coach Park.
Police Force and Tel No: West Midlands (0203 539010)
Disabled Visitors' Facilities
  Wheelchairs: Nicholl Street Stand.
  Blind: No special facility.
Anticipated Development(s): New North Stand roof & New East Stand - construction date unknown.

KEY

- **C** Club Offices
- **S** Club Shop
- **E** Entrance(s) for visiting supporters
- **R** Refreshment bars for visiting supporters
- **T** Toilets for visiting supporters

↑ North direction (approx)

❶ Swan Lane
❷ A4600 Walsgrave Road
❸ Thackhall Street
❹ Coventry BR Station (1 mile)
❺ To M6 Junction 2 and M69
❻ To M45 Junction 1

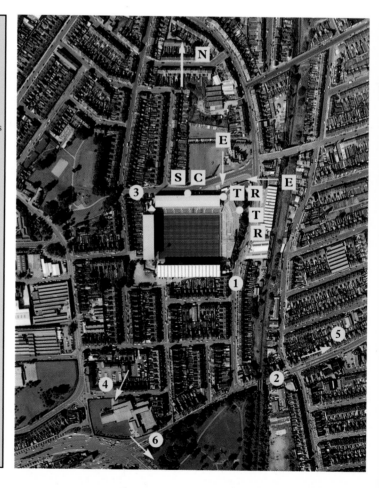

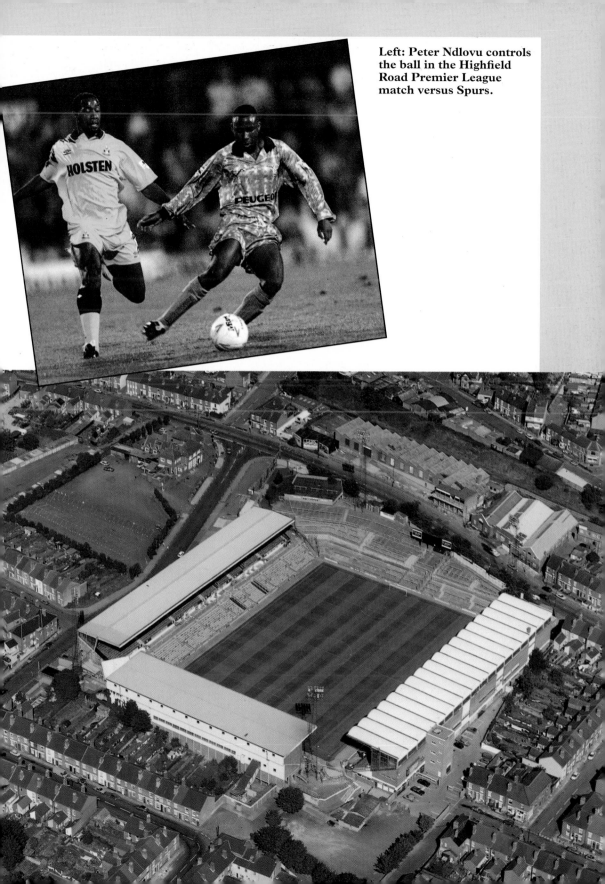

Left: Peter Ndlovu controls the ball in the Highfield Road Premier League match versus Spurs.

CREWE ALEXANDRA

Gresty Road Ground, Crewe, Cheshire, CW2 6EB.

Tel No: 0270 213014
Advance Tickets Tel No: 0270 213014
League: 3rd Division
Brief History: Founded 1877. Former Grounds; Alexandra Recreation ground (Nantwich Road), Earle Street Cricket Ground, Edleston Road, Old Sheds Fields, Gresty Road (Adjacent to current Ground), moved to current Ground in 1906. Founder members of 2nd Division (1892) until 1896. Founder members of 3rd Division North (1921). Record attendance 20,000.
(Total) Current Capacity: 7,200 (1,200 Seated)

Visiting Supporters' Allocation: 1,500
Club Colours: Red Shirts, White Shorts.
Nearest Railway Station: Crewe.
Parking (Car): Car Park at Ground
Parking (Coach/Bus): Car Park at Ground
Police Force and Tel No: Cheshire (0270 500222)
Disabled Visitors' Facilities
  Wheelchairs: Corner Popular Stand/Family area
  Blind: Commentary available

KEY
- **C** Club Offices
- **S** Club Shop
- **E** Entrance(s) for visiting supporters
- **R** Refreshment bars for visiting supporters
- **T** Toilets for visiting supporters

⬆ North direction (approx)

- ❶ Crewe BR Station
- ❷ Car Park
- ❸ Gresty Road
- ❹ A534 Nantwich Road
- ❺ A5020 to M6 Junction 16
- ❻ To M6 Junction 17

Left: Phil Clarkson wins the ball from two Blackburn players, in Crewe's F.A. Cup match with the Rovers.

CRYSTAL PALACE

Selhurst Park, London, SE25 6PU

Tel No: 081 653 4462
Advance Tickets Tel No: 081 771 8841
League: 1st Division
Brief History: Founded 1905. Former Grounds: The Crystal Palace (F.A. Cup Finals venue), London County Athletic Ground (Herne Hill), The Nest (Croydon Common Athletic Ground), moved to Selhurst Park in 1924. Founder members 3rd Division (1920). Record attendance 51,482.
(Total) Current Capacity: 30,115 (15,515 Seated)
Visiting Supporters' Allocation: 5,537 (2,337 Seated)

Club Colours: Red with blue striped shirts, red shorts
Nearest Railway Station: Selhurst, Norwood Junction & Thornton Heath
Parking (Car): Street parking & Sainsbury's car park
Parking (Coach/Bus): Thornton Heath
Police Force and Tel No: Metropolitan (081 653 8568)
Disabled Visitors' Facilities
　Wheelchairs: Park Road Stand (limited)
　Blind: Commentary available

KEY
C Club Offices
S Club Shop
E Entrance(s) for visiting supporters
T Toilets for visiting supporters

↑ North direction (approx)

❶ Whitehorse Lane
❷ Park Road
❸ A213 Selhurst Road
❹ Selhurst BR Station (1/2 mile)
❺ Norwood Junction BR Station
❻ Thornton Heath BR Station (1/2 mile)
❼ Car Park (Sainsbury's)

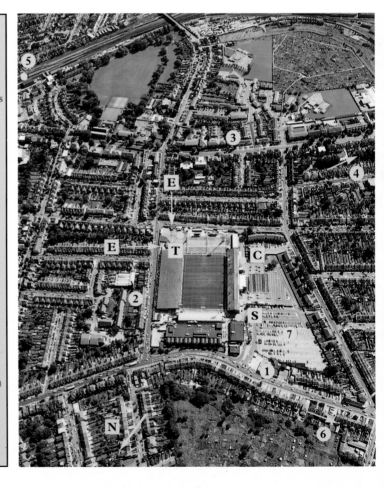

Left: At Selhurst Park, against Leeds United, Chris Armstrong confidently runs with the ball.

DARLINGTON

Feethams Ground, Darlington, DL1 5JB.

Tel No: 0325 465097
Advance Tickets Tel No: 0325 465097
League: 3rd Division
Brief History: Founded 1883. Founder Members of 3rd Division North (1921), Relegated from 4th Division (1989). Promoted from GM Vauxhall Conference in 1990. Record attendance 21,023.
(Total) Current Capacity: 9,957 (1,120 Seated)
Visiting Supporters' Allocation: 1,200 (250 Seated)

Club Colours: White and Black Shirts, Black Shorts.
Nearest Railway Station: Darlington
Parking (Car): Street parking
Parking (Coach/Bus): As directed by Police
Police Force and Tel No: Durham (0325 467681)
Disabled Visitors' Facilities
Wheelchairs: East Stand
Blind: No special facility

KEY

C Club Offices
S Club Shop
E Entrance(s) for visiting supporters
R Refreshment bars for visiting supporters
T Toilets for visiting supporters

↑ North direction (approx)

❶ Polam Lane
❷ Victoria Embankment
❸ Feethams Cricket Ground
❹ Victoria Road
❺ Darlington BR Station (¼ mile)
❻ To A1 (M)

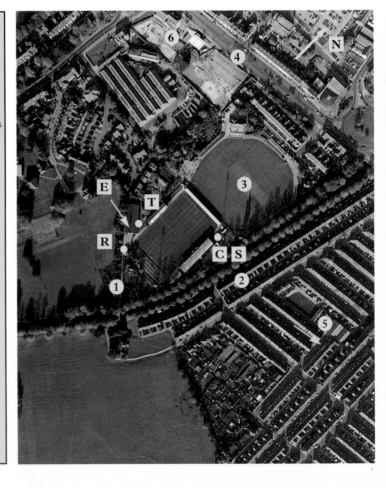

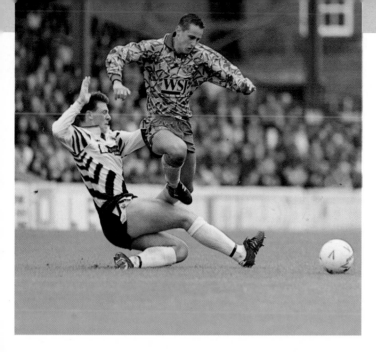

Left: Shrewsbury's Carl Griffiths leaps over the legs of Sean Gregan, as the Darlington player stretches for the ball.

DERBY COUNTY

Baseball Ground, Shaftesbury Crescent, Derby, DE3 8NB

Tel No: 0332 40105
Advance Tickets Tel No: 0332 40105
League: 1st Division
Brief History: Founded 1884. Former Ground: The Racecourse Ground, moved to Baseball Ground in 1894. Founder-members of the Football League (1888). Record attendance 41,826.
(Total) Current Capacity: 23,800 (14,500 Seated)

Club Colours: White shirts, black shorts
Nearest Railway Station: Derby Midland and Ramsline Halt (specials)
Parking (Car): Several car parks
Parking (Coach/Bus): Russel Street
Police Force and Tel No: Derbyshire (0332 290100)
Disabled Visitors' Facilities
  Wheelchairs: Vulcan Street
  Blind: Commentary available

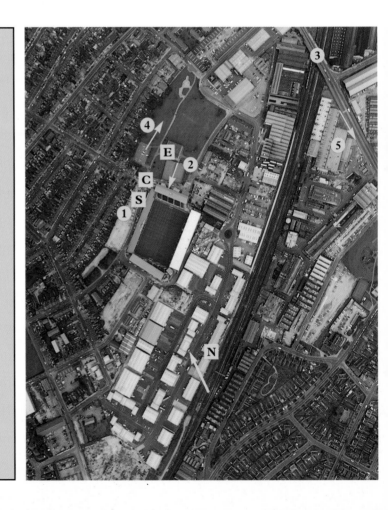

KEY

C Club Offices
S Club Shop
E Entrance(s) for visiting supporters

↑ North direction (approx)

❶ Shaftesbury Crescent
❷ Colombo Street
❸ A514 Osmaston Road
❹ To Derby Midland BR Station (1 mile)
❺ To Ring Road, A6 & M1 Junction 24

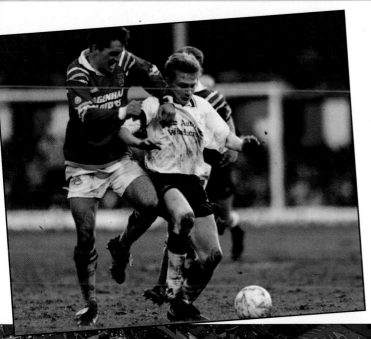

Left: Martin Allen of West Ham tussles with County's Mark Pembridge, in this First Division match.

DONCASTER ROVERS

Belle Vue, Bawtry Road, Doncaster DN4 5HT

Tel No: 0302 539441
Advance Tickets Tel No: 0302 539441
League: 3rd Division
Brief History: Founded 1879. Former Grounds; Town Moor, Belle Vue (not current Ground), Deaf School Playing Field (later name Intake Ground), Bennetthorpe, moved to Belle Vue (former name Low Pasture) in 1922. Record attendance 37,149.
(Total) Current Capacity: 6,535 (1,259 Seated)

Club Colours: White with Red trim Shirts, White Shorts.
Nearest Railway Station: Doncaster
Parking (Car): Car Park at ground
Parking (Coach/Bus): Car Park at ground
Police Force and Tel No: South Yorkshire (0302 366744)
Disabled Visitors' Facilities
    Wheelchairs: Bawtry Road
    Blind: No special facility

KEY
C Club Offices
S Club Shop
E Entrance(s) for visiting supporters
R Refreshment bars for visiting supporters
T Toilets for visiting supporters

↑ North direction (approx)

❶ A638 Bawtry Road
❷ Racecourse
❸ Car Park
❹ To Doncaster BR Station & A1(M) (3 miles)
❺ To A630 & M18 Junction 4

Left: Shane Reddish prepares to take a throw-in, at the Belle Vue match with Shrewsbury.

EVERTON

Goodison Park, Goodison Road, Liverpool, L4 4EL

Tel No: 051 521 2020
Advance Tickets Tel No: 051 521 2020
League: F.A. Premier
Brief History: Founded 1879 as St. Domingo, changed to Everton in 1880. Former Grounds: Stanley Park, Priory Road and Anfield (Liverpool F.C. Ground), moved to Goodison Park in 1892. Founder-members Football League (1888). Record attendance 78,299.
(Total) Current Capacity: 38,500 (36,500 Seated)

Club Colours: Blue shirts, white shorts
Nearest Railway Station: Liverpool Lime Street
Parking (Car): Corner of Utting & Priory Avenues
Parking (Coach/Bus): Priory Road
Police Force and Tel No: Merseyside (051 709 6010)
Disabled Visitors' Facilities
  Wheelchairs: Bullens Road
  Blind: Commentary available

KEY

C Club Offices
S Club Shop
E Entrance(s) for visiting supporters
R Refreshment bars for visiting supporters
T Toilets for visiting supporters

↑ North direction (approx)

❶ A580 Walton Road
❷ Bullens Road
❸ Goodison Road
❹ Car Park
❺ Liverpool Lime Street BR Station (2 miles)
❻ To M57 Junction 2, 4 and 5
❼ Stanley Park

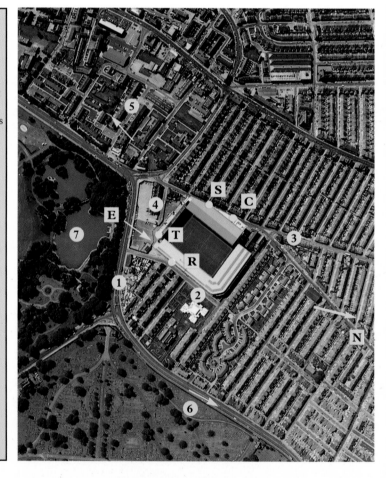

Right: Arguably the World's top goalkeeper, Welsh international Neville Southall, the regular Everton custodian for many years.

EXETER CITY

St. James Park, Exeter, EX4 6PX

Tel No: 0392 54073
Advance Tickets Tel No: 0392 54073
League: 2nd Division
Brief History: Founded in 1904. (From amalgamation of St. Sidwell United and Exeter United) Founder-members Third Division (1920). Record attendance 20,984.
(Total) Current Capacity: 8,898 (1,608 Seated)
Club Colours: Red and white striped shirts, black shorts

Nearest Railway Station: Exeter St. James Park
Parking (Car): National Car Park and Street parking
Parking (Coach/Bus): Paris Street bus station
Police Force and Tel No: Devon and Cornwall (0392 52101)
Disabled Visitors' Facilities
  Wheelchairs: Well Street
  Blind: No special facility

KEY
C Club Offices
S Club Shop
E Entrance(s) for visiting supporters
T Toilets for visiting supporters

↑ North direction (approx)

❶ Exeter St. James Park BR Station
❷ St. James Road
❸ Old Tiverton Road
❹ Blackboy Road

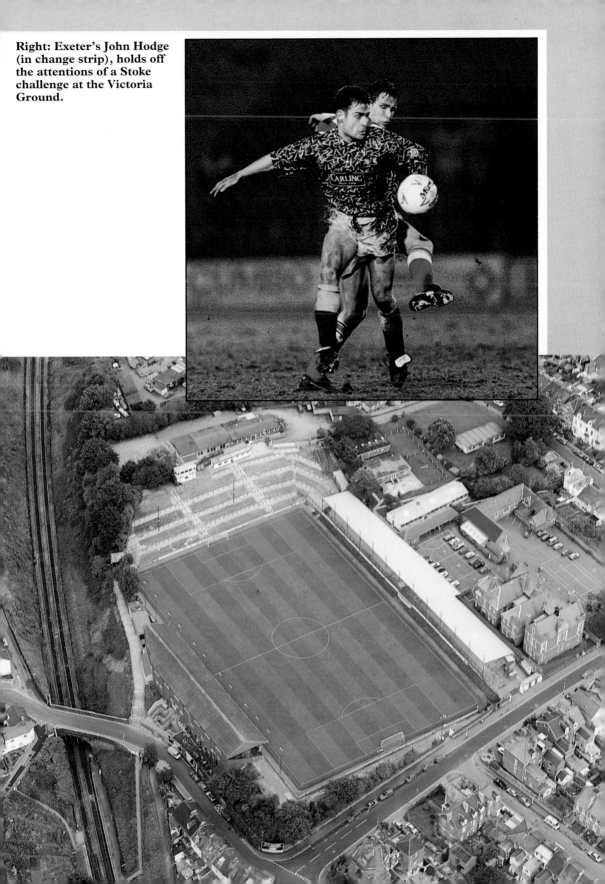

Right: Exeter's John Hodge (in change strip), holds off the attentions of a Stoke challenge at the Victoria Ground.

FULHAM

Craven Cottage, Stevenage Road, Fulham, London, SW6 6HH

Tel No: 071 736 6561
Advance Tickets Tel No: 071 736 6561
League: 2nd Division
Brief History: Founded in 1879 as St. Andrews Fulham, changed name to Fulham in 1898. Former Grounds: Star Road, Ranelagh Club, Lillie Road, Eel Brook Common, Purser's Cross, Barn Elms and Half Moon (then the ground of Wasps Rugby Football Club), moved to Craven Cottage in 1894. Record attendance 49,335.
(Total) Current Capacity: 16,815 (6,600 Seated)

Club Colours: White shirts, black shorts
Nearest Railway Station: Putney Bridge (Tube)
Parking (Car): Street parking
Parking (Coach/Bus): Stevenage Road
Police Force and Tel No: Metropolitan (071 741 6212)
Disabled Visitors' Facilities
Wheelchairs: Miller Stand
Blind: Commentary available (prior arrangement)

KEY
C Club Offices
S Club Shop
E Entrance(s) for visiting supporters
R Refreshment bars for visiting supporters
T Toilets for visiting supporters

↑ North direction (approx)

❶ River Thames
❷ Stevenage Road
❸ Finlay Street
❹ Putney Bridge Tube Station (1/2 mile)
❺ The Cottage

Left: Former Luton Junior Sean Farrell - already a Fulham favourite - in typical aerial combat with Stockport's Jim Gannon.

GILLINGHAM

Priestfield Stadium, Redfern Avenue, Gillingham, Kent, ME7 4DD

Tel No: 0634 851854
Advance Tickets Tel No: 0634 576828
League: 3rd Division
Brief History: Founded 1893, as New Brompton, changed name to Gillingham in 1913. Founder-members Third Division (1920). Lost Football League status (1938), re-elected to Third Division South (1950). Record attendance 23,002.
(Total) Current Capacity: 10,422 (1,225 Seated)

Club Colours: Blue shirts, white shorts
Nearest Railway Station: Gillingham
Parking (Car): Street parking
Parking (Coach/Bus): As directed by Police
Police Force and Tel No: Kent (0634 834488)
Disabled Visitors' Facilities
  Wheelchairs: Redfern Avenue
  Blind: No special facility

KEY
- **C** Club Offices
- **S** Club Shop
- **E** Entrance(s) for visiting supporters
- **R** Refreshment bars for visiting supporters
- **T** Toilets for visiting supporters

↑ North direction (approx)

- ❶ Redfern Avenue
- ❷ Toronto Road
- ❸ Gordon Road
- ❹ Gillingham BR Station (¼ mile)
- ❺ Woodlands Road

Right: Gills' left-sided Gary Breen clears his lines during a Gillingham away match.

GRIMSBY TOWN

Blundell Park, Cleethorpes, DN35 7PY

Tel No: 0472 697111
Advance Tickets Tel No: 0472 697111
League: 1st Division
Brief History: Founded 1878, as Grimsby Pelham, changed name to Grimsby Town in 1879. Former Grounds: Clee Park (two adjacent fields) & Abbey Park, moved to Blundell Park in 1899. Founder-members 2nd Division (1892). Record attendance 31,651.
(Total) Current Capacity: 17,526 (5,021 Seated)

Club Colours: Black & white striped shirts, black shorts
Nearest Railway Station: Cleethorpes & New Clee (specials)
Parking (Car): Street Parking
Parking (Coach/Bus): Harrington Street
Police Force and Tel No: Humberside (0472 697131)
Disabled Visitors' Facilities
 Wheelchairs: Harrington Street
 Blind: Commentary available

KEY

C Club Offices
S Club Shop
E Entrance(s) for visiting supporters
R Refreshment bars for visiting supporters
T Toilets for visiting supporters

↑ North direction (approx)

❶ A180 Grimsby Road
❷ Cleethorpes BR Station (1½ miles)
❸ To Grimsby and M180 Junction 5
❹ Harrington Street
❺ Constitutional Avenue
❻ Humber Estuary
❼ Findus Stand

Left: A familiar sight at Blundell Park, with the ball at his feet, Clive Mendonca bears down on goal.

HARTLEPOOL UNITED

Victoria Ground, Clarence Road, Hartlepool, TS24 8BZ

Tel No: 0429 272584
Advance Tickets Tel No: 0429 222077
League: 2nd Division
Brief History: Founded 1908 as Hartlepools United, changed to Hartlepool (1968) and to Hartlepool United in 1977. Founder-members 3rd Division (1921). Record attendance 17,426.
(Total) Current Capacity: 6,721 (2,316 Seated)
Visiting Supporters' Allocation: 680 (Allocation can be extended to 2,070)

Club Colours: Sky and navy blue shirts, navy blue shorts.
Nearest Railway Station: Hartlepool Church Street
Parking (Car): Street parking and rear of clock garage
Parking (Coach/Bus): United bus station
Police Force and Tel No: Cleveland (0429 221151)
Disabled Visitors' Facilities
  Wheelchairs: Raby Road
  Blind: Commentary available

KEY
- **C** Club Offices
- **S** Club Shop
- **E** Entrance(s) for visiting supporters
- ■

↑ North direction (approx)

❶ A1088 Clarence Road
❷ Hartlepool Church Street BR Station
❸ A179 Raby Road
❹ Greyhound Stadium
❺ To Middlesbrough A689 & A1(M)

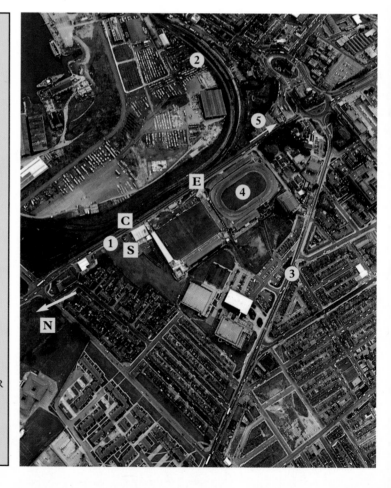

Right: Well experienced John MacPhail seen here in the colours of his latest club - Hartlepool United.

HEREFORD UNITED

Edgar Street, Hereford, HR4 9JU

Tel No: 0432 276666
Advance Tickets Tel No: 0432 276666
League: 3rd Division
Brief History: Founded 1924, elected to Football League 1972. Record attendance 18,114
(Total) Current Capacity: 13,777 (2,897 Seated)
Club Colours: White shirts, black shorts

Nearest Railway Station: Hereford
Parking (Car): Merton Meadow & Edgar Street
Parking (Coach/Bus): Cattle Market
Police Force and Tel No: Hereford (0432 276422)
Disabled Visitors' Facilities
 Wheelchairs: Edgar Street (few)
 Blind: Commentary available

KEY

C Club Offices
S Club Shop
E Entrance(s) for visiting supporters
R Refreshment bars for visiting supporters
T Toilets for visiting supporters

↑ North direction (approx)

❶ A49 Edgar Street
❷ Blackfriars Street
❸ Hereford BR Station (½ mile)
❹ Newmarket Street
❺ To A438 & M50

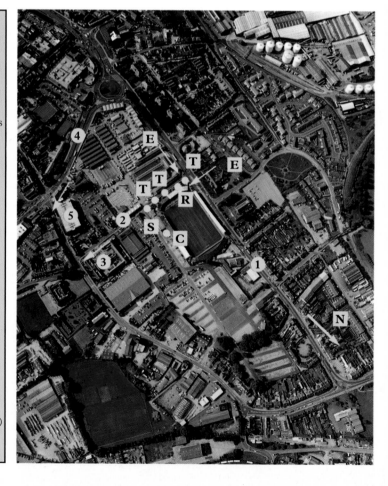

Left: David Titterton in combat with Keith Gillespie of Manchester United, in an attractive pre-season friendly.

HUDDERSFIELD TOWN

Leeds Road, Huddersfield, HD1 6PE

Tel No: 0484 420335
Advance Tickets Tel No: 0484 420335
League: 2nd Division
Brief History: Founded 1908, elected to
Football League in 1910. First Club to win the
Football League Championship three years in
succession. Record attendance 67,037.
(Total) Current Capacity: 17,010 (5,340
Seated)
Visiting Supporters' Allocation: 3,401 (901
Seated)
Club Colours: Blue and white striped shirts,
white shorts
Nearest Railway Station: Huddersfield

Parking (Car): Car parks adjacent to ground
Parking (Coach/Bus): Car parks adjacent to
ground
Police Force and Tel No: West Yorkshire (0484
422122)
Disabled Visitors' Facilities
  Wheelchairs: Bradley Mills Road (special
  raised and covered platform).
  Blind: No special facility
Anticipated Development(s): New stadium
and multi-sport complex (plus Hotel,
Restaurant and Shopping Mall) near to current
Ground, anticipated completion by start of the
1994/95 season.

KEY

C Club Offices
S Club Shop
E Entrance(s) for visiting
supporters
R Refreshment bars for visiting
supporters
T Toilets for visiting supporters

↑ North direction (approx)

❶ A62 Leeds Road
❷ Bradley Mills Road
❸ To Leeds and M62 Junction
25
❹ To Huddersfield BR Station
(1¼ miles)
❺ Car Parks

Right: Iwan Roberts leaps for the ball in the Leeds Road early season match with Bradford City.

HULL CITY

Boothferry Park, Boothferry Road, Hull, HU4 6EU

Tel No: 0482 51119
Advance Tickets Tel No: 0482 51119
League: 2nd Division
Brief History: Founded 1904. Former grounds: The Boulevard (Hull Rugby League Ground), Dairycoates, Anlaby Road Cricket Circle (Hull Cricket Ground), Anlaby Road, moved to Boothferry Park in 1946. Record attendance 55,019.
(Total) Current Capacity: 17,528 (5,515 Seated)
Visiting Supporters' Allocation: 3,260 (530 Seated)

Club Colours: Amber & black striped shirts, black shorts
Nearest Railway Station: Hull Paragon
Parking (Car): Street Parking and at ground (limited)
Parking (Coach/Bus): At ground
Police Force and Tel No: Humberside (0482 220148)
Disabled Visitors' Facilities
   Wheelchairs: Corner East/South stands
   Blind: Commentary available

KEY

C Club Offices
E Entrance(s) for visiting supporters

↑ North direction (approx)

❶ A63 Boothferry Road
❷ North Road
❸ Hull Paragon BR Station (1½ miles)
❹ To Humber Bridge and M62 Junction 38

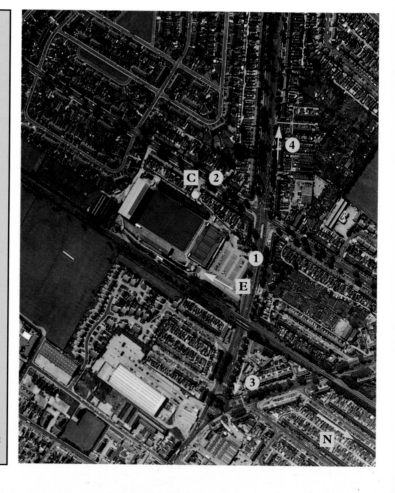

Left: Martin Carruthers is in full control of the ball as a Tigers team-mate looks on.

IPSWICH TOWN

Portman Road, Ipswich IP1 2DA

Telephone: 0473 219211

Advance Tickets Telephone: 0473 221133

League: F.A. Premier

Brief History: Founded 1887 as Ipswich Association F.C., changed to Ipswich Town in 1888. Former Grounds: Broom Hill & Brookes Hall, moved to Portman Road in 1888. Record attendance 38,010

Total Current Capacity: 22,000 (22,000 Seated)

Visiting Supporters Allocation: 1,500 (1,500 Seated)

Club Colours: Blue shirts, white shorts

Nearest Railway Station: Ipswich

Parking (Car): Portman Road & Portman Walk

Parking (Coach/Bus): Portman Walk

Police Force and Tel. No.: Suffolk (0473 611611)

Disabled Visitors Facilities:
Wheelchairs: South Stand (Churchmans)
Blind: Commentary available

KEY

C Club Offices
S Club Shop
E Entrance(s) for visiting supporters
R Refreshment bars for visiting supporters
T Toilets for visiting supporters

↑ North direction (approx)

❶ A137 West End Road
❷ A1071 Handford Road
❸ Portman Road
❹ Princes Street
❺ Ipswich BR Station
❻ Car Parks

Left: Ipswich's Geraint Williams and Spurs' Justin Edinburgh in a midfield tussle early in the 92-93 season.

Below: Veteran Ipswich and Scotland star John Wark celebrates another goal, against Spurs in August 92.

LEEDS UNITED

Elland Road, Leeds, LS11 0ES

Tel No: 0532 716037
Advance Tickets Tel No: 0532 710710
League: F.A. Premier
Brief History: Founded 1919, formed from the former 'Leeds City' Club, who were disbanded following expulsion from the Football League in October 1919. Joined Football League in 1920. Record attendance 57,892
(Total) Current Capacity: 32,000 (16,500 Seated)

Club Colours: White shirts, white shorts
Nearest Railway Station: Leeds City
Parking (Car): Car parks adjacent to ground
Parking (Coach/Bus): As directed by Police
Police Force and Tel No: West Yorkshire (0532 435353)
Disabled Visitors' Facilities
　Wheelchairs: West Stand
　Blind: Commentary available

KEY

C Club Offices
S Club Shop
E Entrance(s) for visiting supporters

↑ North direction (approx)

❶ M621
❷ M621 Junction 2
❸ A643 Elland Road
❹ Lowfields Road
❺ To A58

Right: At Elland Road, both Gary Speed and Lee Chapman outjump Steve Chettle of Nottingham Forest.

LEICESTER CITY

City Stadium, Filbert Street, Leicester, LE2 7FL

Tel No: 0533 555000
Advance Tickets Tel No: 0533 555000
League: 1st Division
Brief History: Founded 1884 as Leicester Fosse, changed name to Leicester City in 1919. Former Grounds: Fosse Road South, Victoria Road, Belgrave Cycle Track, Mill Lane & Aylestone Road Cricket Ground, moved to Filbert Street in 1891. Record attendance 47,298
(Total) Current Capacity: 22,181 (12,833 Seated)

Club Colours: Blue shirts, blue shorts
Nearest Railway Station: Leicester
Parking (Car): NCP car park & street parking
Parking (Coach/Bus): Western Boulevard
Police Force and Tel No: Leicester (0533 530066)
Disabled Visitors' Facilities
 Wheelchairs: Filbert Street
 Blind: No special facility
Anticipated Development(s): Re-development of main (members) stand in 1993, which will incorporate improved areas for disabled.

KEY

C Club Offices
S Club Shop
E Entrance(s) for visiting supporters
R Refreshment bars for visiting supporters
T Toilets for visiting supporters

↑ North direction (approx)

❶ Walnut Street
❷ Filbert Street
❸ Grasmere Street
❹ River Soar
❺ M1 and M69 Junction 21
❻ Leicester BR Station (1 mile)

**Right: Well travelled
Bobby Davidson leaves
Brentford defender Keith
Millen in his wake in this
Filbert Street encounter.**

LEYTON ORIENT

Leyton Stadium, Brisbane Road, Leyton, London, E10 5NE

Tel No: 081 539 2223
Advance Tickets Tel No: 081 539 2223
League: 2nd Division
Brief History: Founded 1887 as Clapton Orient, from Eagle Cricket Club (formerly Glyn Cricket Club formed in 1881). Changed name to Leyton Orient (1946), Orient (1966), Leyton Orient (1987). Former grounds: Glyn Road, Whittles Athletic Ground, Millfields Road, Lea Bridge Road, Wembley Stadium (2 games), moved to Brisbane Road in 1937. Record attendance 34,345.
(Total) Current Capacity: 18,869 (7,171 Seated)

Club Colours: Red shirts, white shorts
Nearest Railway Station: Leyton (tube), Leyton Midland Road
Parking (Car): NCP Brisbane Road & street parking
Parking (Coach/Bus): As directed by Police
Police Force and Tel No: Metropolitan (081 556 8855)
Disabled Visitors' Facilities
  Wheelchairs: Windsor Road
  Blind: No special facility

KEY
- **C** Club Offices
- **S** Club Shop
- **E** Entrance(s) for visiting supporters
- **R** Refreshment bars for visiting supporters
- **T** Toilets for visiting supporters

↑ North direction (approx)

❶ Buckingham Road
❷ Oliver Road
❸ A112 High Road Leyton
❹ Leyton Tube Station (¼ mile)
❺ Brisbane Road

Left: Sam Kitchen looks confident at Brisbane Road, on the pitch that was voted as having the best playing surface in the League.

LINCOLN CITY

Sincil Bank, Lincoln, LN5 8LD

Tel No: 0522 522224
Advance Tickets Tel No: 0522 522224
League: 3rd Division
Brief History: Founded 1884. Former Ground: John O'Gaunts Ground, moved to Sincil Bank in 1895. Founder-members 2nd Division Football League (1892). Relegated from 4th Division in 1987, promoted from GM Vauxhall Conference in 1988. Record attendance 23,196.
(Total) Current Capacity: 12,428 (3,271 Seated)
Visiting Supporters' Allocation: 3,716 (641 Seated)

Club Colours: Red & white striped shirts, black shorts
Nearest Railway Station: Lincoln Central
Parking (Car): Adjacent Ground
Parking (Coach/Bus): South Common
Police Force and Tel No: Lincolnshire (0522 529911)
Disabled Visitors' Facilities
  Wheelchairs: South Park Stand
  Blind: No special facility
Anticipated Development(s): Sincil Bank Terrace (home & visiting supporters) to be redeveloped approx. 1994.

KEY

C Club Offices
S Club Shop
E Entrance(s) for visiting supporters
R Refreshment bars for visiting supporters
T Toilets for visiting supporters

⬆ North direction (approx)

❶ A46 High Street
❷ Sincil Bank
❸ Sausthorpe Street
❹ Cross Street
❺ A158 Canwick Road
❻ A158 South Park Avenue
❼ Car Park
❽ Lincoln Central BR Station (½ mile)

Left: Jason Kabia shrugs off the challenge in this 3rd Division match at Sincil Bank.

LIVERPOOL

Anfield Road, Liverpool, L4 0TH

Tel No: 051 263 2361
Advance Tickets Tel No: 051 260 8680
League: F.A. Premier
Brief History: Founded 1892. Anfield Ground formerly Everton F.C. Ground. Joined Football League in 1893. Record attendance 61,905.
(Total) Current Capacity: 44,431 (27,951 Seated)
Visiting Supporters' Allocation: 3,059 (3,059 Seated)
Club Colours: Red shirts, red shorts
Nearest Railway Station: Kirkdale

Parking (Car): Stanley car park
Parking (Coach/Bus): Priory Road & Pinehurst Avenue
Police Force and Tel No: Merseyside (051 709 6010)
Disabled Visitors' Facilities
Wheelchairs: Lothair Road
Blind: Commentary available
Anticipated Development(s): Spion Kop Terrace to be developed to approx. 10,000 seats - 1993/94 season.

KEY

C Club Offices
S Club Shop
E Entrance(s) for visiting supporters

⬆ North direction (approx)

❶ Car Park
❷ Anfield Road
❸ A5089 Walton Breck Road
❹ Kemlyn Road
❺ Kirkdale BR Station (1 mile)
❻ Utting Avenue
❼ Stanley Park
❽ Spion Kop

Right: The fourth goal against Chesterfield equals Roger Hunt's individual Liverpool goal scoring record for Ian Rush.

LUTON TOWN

Kenilworth Road Stadium, 1 Maple Road, Luton, LU4 8AW

Tel No: 0582 411622
Advance Tickets Tel No: 0582 30748
League: 1st Division
Brief History: Founded 1885 from an amalgamation of Wanderers F.C. & Excelsior F.C. Former Grounds: Dallow Lane & Dunstable Road, moved to Kenilworth Road in 1905. Record attendance 30,069.
(Total) Current Capacity: 13,374 (9,116 Seated)
Club Colours: White shirts with royal blue & orange stripe on collar & waist. Royal blue shorts with white & orange trim.

Nearest Railway Station: Luton

Parking (Car): Street parking

Parking (Coach/Bus): Luton bus station

Police Force and Tel No: Bedfordshire (0582 401212)

Disabled Visitors' Facilities
Wheelchairs: Maple Road
Blind: Commentary available

KEY
C Club Offices
S Club Shop
E Entrance(s) for visiting supporters
R Refreshment bars for visiting supporters
T Toilets for visiting supporters

↑ North direction (approx)

❶ To M1 Junction 11
❷ Wimborne Road
❸ Kenilworth Road
❹ Oak Road
❺ Dunstable Road (Ring Road)
❻ Luton BR Station (1 mile)

Left: Luton's Paul Telfer looks on, in the 1st Division encounter with Birmingham City at St Andrews.

MANCHESTER CITY

Maine Road, Moss Side, Manchester, M14 7WN

Tel No: 061 226 1191
Advance Tickets Tel No: 061 226 2224
League: F.A. Premier
Brief History: Founded 1880 as West Gorton, changed name to Ardwick (reformed 1887) and to Manchester City in 1894. Former grounds: Clowes Street, Kirkmanshulme Cricket Club, Donkey Common, Pink Bank Lane & Hyde Road, moved to Maine Road in 1923. Founder-members 2nd Division (1892). Record attendance 84,569 (record for Football League ground).
(Total) Current Capacity: Approaching 40,000 (21,500 Seated)
Visiting Supporters' Allocation: 4,465 (1,251 Seated) May be varied according to arrangements with Police.

Club Colours: Sky blue shirts, white shorts
Nearest Railway Station: Manchester Piccadilly (2½ miles)
Parking (Car): Street parking & local schools
Parking (Coach/Bus): Kippax Street car park
Police Force and Tel No: Greater Manchester (061 872 5050)
Disabled Visitors' Facilities
   Wheelchairs: Platt Lane
   Blind: No special facility
Anticipated Development(s): Seating of Kippax Street Stand during 1994 close season.

KEY
C Club Offices
S Club Shop
E Entrance(s) for visiting supporters

⬆ North direction (approx)

❶ Thornton Road
❷ South Upper Lloyd Street
❸ To A5103 Princess Road
❹ To City Centre and Manchester Piccadilly BR Station (2½ miles)
❺ To A6010 & M31 Junction 7
❻ Maine Road

Left: Gary Flitcroft receiving congratulations after another City goal.

MANCHESTER UNITED

Old Trafford, Warwick Road North, Manchester, M16 0RA

Tel No: 061 872 1661
Advance Tickets Tel No: 061 872 0199
League: F.A. Premier
Brief History: Founded in 1878 as 'Newton Heath L & Y', later Newton Heath, changed to Manchester United in 1902. Former Grounds: North Road, Monsall & Bank Street, Clayton, moved to Old Trafford in 1910 (used Manchester City F.C. Ground 1941-49). Founder-members Second Division (1892). Record attendance 76,962.
(Total) Current Capacity: 34,266 (30,700 Seated) (Temporary capacities)

Club Colours: Red shirts, white shorts
Nearest Railway Station: At Ground
Parking (Car): Lancashire Cricket Ground & White City
Parking (Coach/Bus): As directed by Police
Police Force and Tel No: Greater Manchester (061 872 5050)
Disabled Visitors' Facilities
 Wheelchairs: In front of Main Stand.
 Blind: Commentary available '

KEY
C Club Offices
S Club Shop

↑ North direction (approx)

❶ A5081 Trafford Park Road to M63 Junction 4 (5 miles)
❷ A56 Chester Road
❸ Manchester Ship Canal
❹ Old Trafford Cricket Ground
❺ To Parking and Warwick Road BR Station

Right: Brian McClair, Mark Hughes and Ryan Giggs celebrate another United goal, against Forest in January '93.

MANSFIELD TOWN

Field Mill Ground, Quarry Lane, Mansfield, Notts

Tel No: 0623 23567
Advance Tickets Tel No: 0623 23567
League: 3rd Division
Brief History: Founded 1910 as Mansfield Wesleyans Boys Brigade, changed to Mansfield Town in 1914. Former Grounds: Pelham Street, Newgate Lane & The Prairie, moved to Field Mill in 1919. Record attendance 24,467.
(Total) Current Capacity: 10,315 (3,448 Seated)
Club Colours: Amber with blue trim shirts, royal blue and amber shorts

Nearest Railway Station: Mansfield Alfreton Parkway (9 miles)
Parking (Car): Car park at Ground
Parking (Coach/Bus): Car park at Ground
Police Force and Tel No: Nottinghamshire (0623 22622)
Disabled Visitors' Facilities
 Wheelchairs: Bishop Street (Entrance at North end of West stand)
 Blind: No special facility

KEY
C Club Offices
E Entrance(s) for visiting supporters

↑ North direction (approx)

❶ Car Park
❷ Quarry Lane
❸ A60 Nottingham Road to M1 Junction 27
❹ Portland Street
❺ To A38 and M1 Junction 28
❻ Town Centre

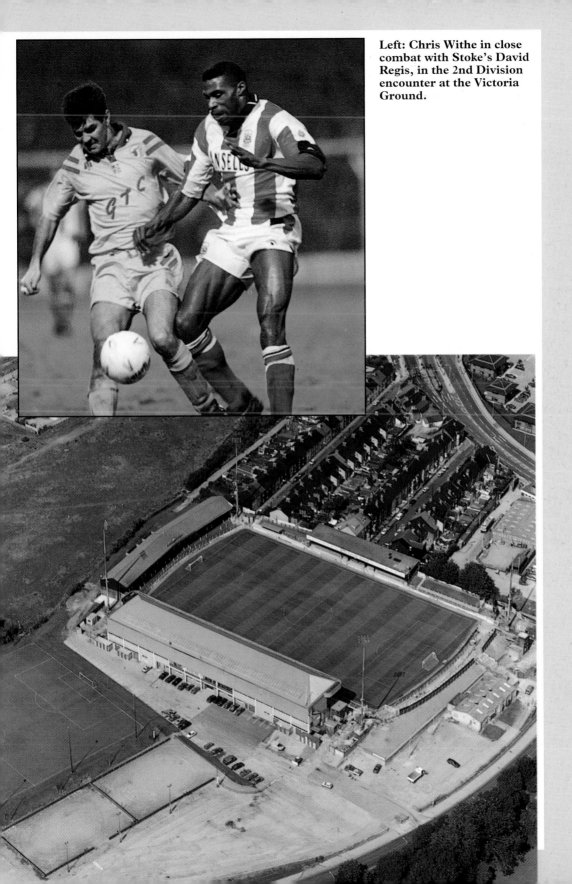

Left: Chris Withe in close combat with Stoke's David Regis, in the 2nd Division encounter at the Victoria Ground.

MIDDLESBROUGH

Ayresome Park, Middlesbrough, Cleveland, TS1 4PB

Tel No: 0642 819659
Advance Tickets Tel No: 0642 815996
League: 1st Division
Brief History: Founded 1876. Former Grounds: Archery Ground (Albert Park), Breckon Hill Road, Linthorpe Road, moved to Ayresome Park in 1903. F.A. Amateur Cup winners 1894 & 1897 (joined Football League in 1899). Record attendance 53,596
(Total) Current Capacity: 26,677 (13,146 Seated)
Visiting Supporters' Allocation: 2,342 (502 Seated)

Club Colours: Red shirts with white yoke, white shorts
Nearest Railway Station: Middlesbrough
Parking (Car): Street parking
Parking (Coach/Bus): As directed by Police
Police Force and Tel No: Cleveland (0642 248184)
Disabled Visitors' Facilities
  Wheelchairs: Corner Ayresome Street/Ayresome Park Road
  Blind: Commentary available
Anticipated Development(s): All-seater fully covered stadium by 1995/96 season.

KEY
- **C** Club Offices
- **S** Club Shop
- **E** Entrance(s) for visiting supporters
- **R** Refreshment bars for visiting supporters
- **T** Toilets for visiting supporters

↑ North direction (approx)

- ❶ Ayresome Street
- ❷ Ayresome Park Road
- ❸ Linthorpe Road
- ❹ Middlesbrough BR Station (1 mile) and Town Centre

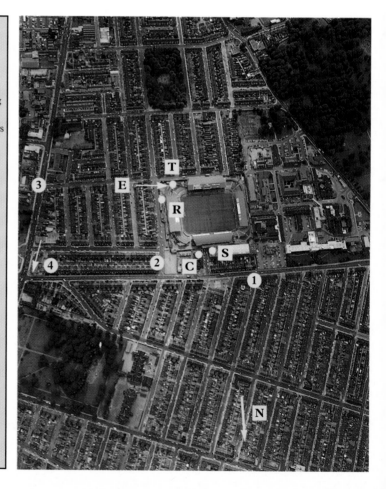

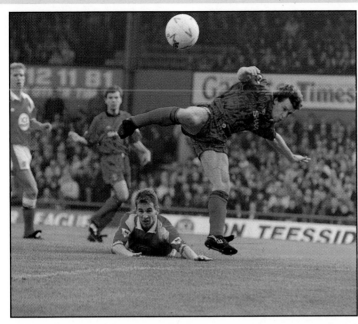

Left: Chris Morris is left on the ground, as Manchester United's Mark Hughes attempts to make contact with the ball.

MILLWALL

New Den, Bolina Road, London, SE16

Tel No: 071 232 1222
Advance Tickets Tel No: 071 231 9999
League: 1st Division
Brief History: Founded 1885 as Millwall
Rovers, changed name to Millwall Athletic
(1889) and Millwall (1925). Former Grounds:
Glengall Road, East Ferry Road (2 separate
Grounds), North Greenwich Ground and The
Den - Cold Blow Lane - moved to New Den
1993/94 season. Founder-members Third
Division (1920). Record attendance (at The
Den) 48,672.

(Total) Current Capacity: 20,150 (20,150
Seated)
Club Colours: Blue shirts, white shorts
Nearest Railway Station: South Bermondsey
BR or Surrey Quays (tube)
Parking (Car): At Ground
Parking (Coach/Bus): At Ground
Police Force and Tel No: Metropolitan
(071 679 9217)
Disabled Visitors' Facilities
  Wheelchairs: Main (West) Stand
  Blind: Main (West) Stand

KEY

C Club Offices
S Club Shop
E Entrance(s) for visiting
supporters
R Refreshment bars for visiting
supporters
T Toilets for visiting supporters

↑ North direction (approx)

❶ Bolina Road
❷ South Bermondsey BR
❸ Surrey Quays Underground
❹ Rotherhithe Tunnel
❺ Ilderton Road
❻ The 'Old' Den
❼ River Thames

Left: The Lions' Andy Roberts and Sunderland's Shaun Cunnington battle for the ball, in the match at Roker Park.

NEWCASTLE UNITED

St. James Park, Newcastle-upon-Tyne, NE1 4ST

Tel No: 091 232 8361
Advance Tickets Tel No: 091 261 1571
League: F. A. Premier
Brief History: Founded in 1882 as Newcastle East End, changed to Newcastle United in 1892. Former Grounds: Chillingham Road, moved to St. James Park (former home of defunct Newcastle West End) in 1892. Record attendance 68,386.
(Total) Current Capacity: 30,348 (11,725 Seated)

Club Colours: Black & white striped shirts, black shorts
Nearest Railway Station: Newcastle Central
Parking (Car): Leazes car park & street parking
Parking (Coach/Bus): Leazes car park
Police Force and Tel No: Northumbria (091 232 3451)
Disabled Visitors' Facilities
  Wheelchairs: Leazes End
  Blind: Commentary available

KEY

C Club Offices
E Entrance(s) for visiting supporters

⬆ North direction (approx)

❶ St. James Street
❷ Strawberry Place
❸ Gallowgate
❹ Wellington Street
❺ To Newcastle Central BR Station (½ mile) & A6127 (M)
❻ Car Park

Left: Stylish Steve Howey exhibiting the defensive qualities that helped Newcastle to the Division 1 title.

NORTHAMPTON TOWN

County Ground, Abington Avenue, Northampton, NN1 4PS

Tel No: 0604 234100
Advance Tickets Tel No: 0604 234100
League: 3rd Division
Brief History: Founded 1897. Ground is part of Northamptonshire County Cricket Ground. Record attendance 24,523
(Total) Current Capacity: 9,443 (360 Seated)
Club Colours: White with claret trim shirts, white with claret trim shorts
Nearest Railway Station: Northampton Castle

Parking (Car): Street parking
Parking (Coach/Bus): Abington Park
Police Force and Tel No: Northants (0604 33221)
Disabled Visitors' Facilities
   Wheelchairs: Cricket pitch side
   Blind: No special facility
Anticipated Development(s): Anticipated relocation in 1995 to a new stadium.

KEY
C Club Offices
S Club Shop
E Entrance(s) for visiting supporters
R Refreshment bars for visiting supporters
T Toilets for visiting supporters

↑ North direction (approx)

❶ Abington Avenue
❷ A5101 Park Avenue North
❸ A45 Wellingborough Road
❹ Park Avenue South
❺ Remainder of County Cricket Ground
❻ Northampton Castle BR Station (2 miles)

Right: Terry Angus, together with Kevin Wilkin and Ian MacParland form the defensive wall at the County Ground.

NORWICH CITY

Carrow Road, Norwich, NR1 1JE

Tel No: 0603 612131
Advance Tickets Tel No: 0603 761661
League: F.A. Premier
Brief History: Founded 1902. Former grounds: Newmarket Road and the Nest, Rosary Road; moved to Carrow Road in 1935. Founder members 3rd Division (1920). Record attendance 43,984.
(Total) Current Capacity: 20,559 (20,559 Seated)

Club Colours: Yellow shirts, green shorts
Nearest Railway Station: Norwich
Parking (Car): City centre car parks
Parking (Coach/Bus): Lower Clarence Road
Police Force and Tel No: Norfolk (0603 621212)
Disabled Visitors' Facilities
　Wheelchairs: South Stand (heated)
　Blind: No special facility

KEY
C Club Offices
S Club Shop
E Entrance(s) for visiting supporters

↑ North direction (approx)

❶ Carrow Road
❷ A47 King Street
❸ River Wensum
❹ Riverside
❺ Car Park
❻ Norwich BR Station

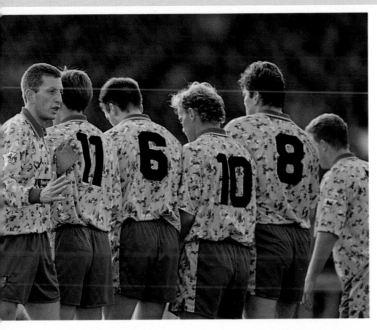

Left: Ian Crook makes the final adjustment to the Norwich wall in this Carrow Road encounter with Middleborough.

NOTTINGHAM FOREST

City Ground, Nottingham, NG2 5FJ

Tel No: 0602 822202
Advance Tickets Tel No: 0602 813801
League: 1st Division
Brief History: Founded 1865 as Forest Football Club, changed name to Nottingham Forest (c.1879). Former Grounds: Forest Recreation Ground, Meadow Cricket Ground, Trent Bridge (Cricket Ground), Parkside, Gregory Ground & Town Ground, moved to City Ground in 1898. Founder-members of Second Division (1892). Record attendance 49,945.

(Total) Current Capacity: 31,091 (15,114 Seated)
Club Colours: Red shirts, white shorts
Nearest Railway Station: Nottingham Midland
Parking (Car): East car park & street parking
Parking (Coach/Bus): East car park
Police Force and Tel No: Nottinghamshire (0602 481888)
Disabled Visitors' Facilities
  Wheelchairs: Front of Executive Stand
  Blind: No special facility

KEY
C Club Offices
S Club Shop
E Entrance(s) for visiting supporters

↑ North direction (approx)

❶ Radcliffe Road
❷ Lady Bay Bridge Road
❸ Trent Bridge
❹ Trent Bridge Cricket Ground
❺ Notts County F.C.
❻ River Trent
❼ Nottingham Midland BR Station (1/2 mile)

Left: Nigel Clough gets to the ball first, despite the close attention of Wimbledon's Vinnie Jones.

NOTTS COUNTY

Meadow Lane, Nottingham, NG2 3HJ

Tel No: 0602 861155
Advance Tickets Tel No: 0602 850632
League: 1st Division
Brief History: Founded 1862 (oldest club in Football League) as Nottingham, changed to Notts County in c.1882. Former Grounds: Notts Cricket Ground (Beeston), Castle Cricket Ground, Trent Bridge Cricket Ground, moved to Meadow Lane in 1910. Founder-members Football League (1888). Record attendance 47,310.
(Total) Current Capacity: 19,241 (16,201 Seated)

Visiting Supporters' Allocation: Up to 5,440 (5,440 Seated)
Club Colours: Black & white stripes, amber sleeves & trim shirts, black shorts.
Nearest Railway Station: Nottingham Midland
Parking (Car): Mainly street parking
Parking (Coach/Bus): Cattle market
Police Force and Tel No: Nottingham (0602 481888)
Disabled Visitors' Facilities
  Wheelchairs: County Road/Meadow Lane
  Blind: No special facility

KEY
- **C** Club Offices
- **S** Club Shop
- **E** Entrance(s) for visiting supporters
- **R** Refreshment bars for visiting supporters
- **T** Toilets for visiting supporters

↑ North direction (approx)

- **❶** A6011 Meadow Lane
- **❷** County Road
- **❸** A60 London Road
- **❹** River Trent
- **❺** Nottingham Midland BR Station (¹/₂ mile)

Right: Northern Ireland international Kevin Wilson (on the right) in combat with Watford's Keith Dublin.

OLDHAM ATHLETIC

Boundary Park, Oldham, OL1 2PA

Tel No: 061 624 4972
Advance Tickets Tel No: 061 624 4972
League: F.A. Premier
Brief History: Founded 1897 as Pine Villa, changed name to Oldham Athletic in 1899. Former Grounds: Berry's Field, Pine Mill, Athletic Ground (later named Boundary Park), Hudson Fold, moved to Boundary Park in 1906. Record attendance 47,671.
(Total) Current Capacity: 16,700 (11,100 Seated)

Club Colours: Blue shirts, blue shorts
Nearest Railway Station: Oldham Werneth
Parking (Car): Lookers Stand car park
Parking (Coach/Bus): At Ground
Police Force and Tel No: Greater Manchester (061 624 0444)
Disabled Visitors' Facilities
  Wheelchairs: Lookers Stand
  Blind: Commentary available

KEY

C Club Offices
E Entrance(s) for visiting supporters

⬆ North direction (approx)

❶ A663 Broadway
❷ Furtherwood Road
❸ Chadderton Way
❹ To A627(M) and M62
❺ To Oldham Werneth BR Station (1½ miles)
❻ Car Park

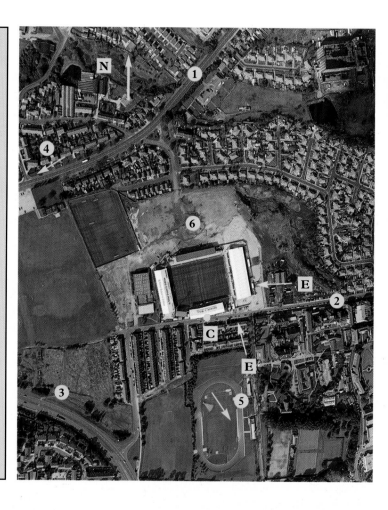

Left: Mike Milligan, following a spell with Everton, is on the ball for Oldham in the Blackburn Rovers match.

OXFORD UNITED

Manor Ground, London Road, Headington, Oxford, OX3 7RS

Tel No: 0865 61503
Advance Tickets Tel No: 0865 61503
League: 1st Division
Brief History: Founded 1893 as Headington (later Headington United), changed name to Oxford United in 1960. Former grounds: Brittania Inn Field, Headington Quarry, Wooten's Field, Manor Ground, The Paddocks, moved back to Manor Ground in 1925. Record attendance 22,730.
(Total) Current Capacity: 11,071 (2,777 Seated)

Club Colours: Yellow with navy trim shirts, navy with yellow trim shorts.
Nearest Railway Station: Oxford (3 miles)
Parking (Car): Street parking
Parking (Coach/Bus): Headley Way
Police Force and Tel No: Thames Valley (0865 777501)
Disabled Visitors' Facilities
  Wheelchairs: Beech Road
  Blind: No special facility

KEY

C Club Offices
S Club Shop
E Entrance(s) for visiting supporters
R Refreshment bars for visiting supporters

↑ North direction (approx)

❶ A420 London Road
❷ Osler Road
❸ To City Centre and Oxford BR Station (3 miles)
❹ To A40 and Ring Road (³/₄ mile)

122

Right: Andrew Melville celebrates an Oxford goal, but the Luton Town fans in the background are not so happy.

PETERBOROUGH UNITED

London Road, Peterborough, Cambs, PE2 8AL

Tel No: 0733 63947
Advance Tickets Tel No: 0733 63947
League: 1st Division
Brief History: Founded in 1934, (no connection with former 'Peterborough and Fletton United' FC). Elected to Football League in 1960. Record attendance 30,096.
(Total) Current Capacity: 16,414 (3,500 Seated)

Club Colours: Blue shirts, white shorts
Nearest Railway Station: Peterborough
Parking (Car): At ground
Parking (Coach/Bus): At ground
Police Force and Tel No: Cambridgeshire (0733 63232)
Disabled Visitors' Facilities
  Wheelchairs: East Stand
  Blind: No special facility

KEY

C Club Offices
S Club Shop
E Entrance(s) for visiting supporters
R Refreshment bars for visiting supporters
T Toilets for visiting supporters

↑ North direction (approx)

❶ A15 London Road
❷ Car Parks
❸ Peterborough BR Station (1 mile)
❹ Glebe Road
❺ A605
❻ To A1 (5 miles)

Right: Posh player Marcus Ebdon nearly loses his shirt in this Division 1 encounter at Notts County.

PLYMOUTH ARGYLE

Home Park, Plymouth, PL2 3DQ

Tel No: 0752 562561
Advance Tickets Tel No: 0752 562561
League: 2nd Division
Brief History: Founded 1886 as Argyle Athletic Club, changed name to Plymouth Argyle in 1903. Founder-members Third Division (1920). Record attendance 43,596
(Total) Current Capacity: 19,900 (6,700 Seated)
Club Colours: Green & white striped shirts, black shorts
Nearest Railway Station: Plymouth
Parking (Car): Car park adjacent
Parking (Coach/Bus): Central car park
Police Force and Tel No: Devon & Cornwall (0752 701188)
Disabled Visitors' Facilities
  Wheelchairs: Devonport End
  Blind: Commentary available

KEY

C Club Offices
S Club Shop
E Entrance(s) for visiting supporters
R Refreshment bars for visiting supporters
T Toilets for visiting supporters

↑ North direction (approx)

❶ Outland Road
❷ Car Park
❸ Devonport Road
❹ Central Park
❺ Town Centre & Plymouth BR Station (¾ mile)

Left: Former Leyton Orient favourite Kevin Nugent, in an aerial duel with John Wark of Ipswich during an F.A.Cup match.

PORTSMOUTH

Fratton Park, 57 Frogmore Road, Portsmouth, Hants, PO4 8RA

Tel No: 0705 731204
Advance Tickets Tel No: 0705 750825
League: 1st Division
Brief History: Founded 1898. Founder-members Third Division (1920). Record attendance 51,385.
(Total) Current Capacity: 26,452 (6,652 Seated)
Visiting Supporters' Allocation: 5,848 (1,228 Seated)
Club Colours: Blue shirts, white shorts

Nearest Railway Station: Fratton
Parking (Car): Street parking
Parking (Coach/Bus): As directed by Police
Police Force and Tel No: Hampshire (0705 321111)
Disabled Visitors' Facilities
  Wheelchairs: Frogmore Road
  Blind: No special facility
Anticipated Development(s): Seeking Ground re-location.

KEY

- **C** Club Offices
- **S** Club Shop
- **E** Entrance(s) for visiting supporters
- **R** Refreshment bars for visiting supporters
- **T** Toilets for visiting supporters

↑ North direction (approx)

- ❶ Alverstone Road
- ❷ Carisbrook Road
- ❸ A288 Milton Road
- ❹ A2030 Eastern Road to A27
- ❺ A2030 Goldsmith Avenue
- ❻ Fratton BR Station (½ mile)

Left: Pompey's talented England international Mark Chamberlain - considered by many as still to realise his true potential.

PORT VALE

Vale Park, Burslem, Stoke-on-Trent, ST6 1AW

Tel No: 0782 814134
Advance Tickets Tel No: 0782 814134
League: 2nd Division
Brief History: Founded 1876 as Burslem Port
Vale, changed name to 'Port Vale' in 1907
(reformed club). Former Grounds: The
Meadows Longport, Moorland Road Athletic
Ground, Cobridge Athletic Grounds,
Recreation Ground Hanley, moved to Vale
Park in 1950. Founder-members Second
Division (1892). Record attendance 50,000.

(Total) Current Capacity: 22,359 (12,442
Seated)
Club Colours: White shirts, black shorts
Nearest Railway Station: Longport or Stoke
Parking (Car): Car park at Ground
Parking (Coach/Bus): Hamil Road car park
Police Force and Tel No: Staffordshire (0782
577114)
Disabled Visitors' Facilities
　Wheelchairs: Lorne Street
　Blind: Commentary available

KEY
C Club Offices
E Entrance(s) for visiting
supporters

↑ North direction (approx)

❶ Car Parks
❷ Hamil Road
❸ Longport BR Station (1 mile)
❹ Lorne Street
❺ B5051 Moorland Road

Left: Keith Houchen, Nicky Cross and Dean Glover, all look pleased during the home match with Plymouth.

PRESTON NORTH END

Lowthorpe Road, Deepdale, PR1 6RU

Tel No: 0772 795919
Advance Tickets Tel No: 0772 795919
League: 3rd Division
Brief History: Founded 1867 as a Rugby Club, changed to soccer in 1881. Former ground: Moor park, moved to (later named) Deepdale in 1875. Founder-members Football League (1888). Record attendance 42,684.
(Total) Current Capacity: 16,500 (3,000 Seated)

Club Colours: White shirts, blue shorts
Nearest Railway Station: Preston (2 miles)
Parking (Car): West Stand car park
Parking (Coach/Bus): West Stand car park
Police Force and Tel No: Lancashire (0772 203203)
Disabled Visitors' Facilities
  Wheelchairs: Deepdale Road
  Blind: No special facility

KEY
C Club Offices
S Club Shop
E Entrance(s) for visiting supporters
R Refreshment bars for visiting supporters
T Toilets for visiting supporters

↑ North direction (approx)

❶ A6033 Deepdale Road
❷ Lowthorpe Road
❸ Car Park
❹ A5085 Blackpool Road
❺ Preston BR Station (2 miles)
❻ Fulwood End – Spion Kop

Left: Lee Cartwright gets to the ball first, despite the close attention of Stockport's David Frain.

QUEENS PARK RANGERS

Rangers Stadium, South Africa Road, London, W12 7PA

Tel No: 081 743 0262
Advance Tickets Tel No: 081 749 5744
League: F.A. Premier
Brief History: Founded 1885 as 'St. Jude's Institute', amalgamated with Christchurch Rangers to become Queens Park Rangers in 1886. Football League record number of former Grounds and Ground moves (13 different venues, 17 changes), including White City Stadium (twice) final move to Rangers Stadium (then named Loftus Road) in 1963. Founder-members Third Division (1920). Record attendance 35,353.
(Total) Current Capacity: 23,480 (15,026 Seated)

Club Colours: Blue & white hooped shirts, white shorts

Nearest Railway Station: Shepherds Bush and White City (both tube)

Parking (Car): White City NCP & street parking

Parking (Coach/Bus): White City NCP

Police Force and Tel No: Metropolitan (081 741 6212)

Disabled Visitors' Facilities
   Wheelchairs: Ellerslie Road
   Blind: No special facility

KEY

C Club Offices
S Club Shop
E Entrance(s) for visiting supporters

↑ North direction (approx)

❶ South Africa Road
❷ To White City Tube Station, A219 Wood Lane and A40 Western Avenue
❸ A4020 Uxbridge Road
❹ To Shepherds Bush Tube Station
❺ Ellerslie Road

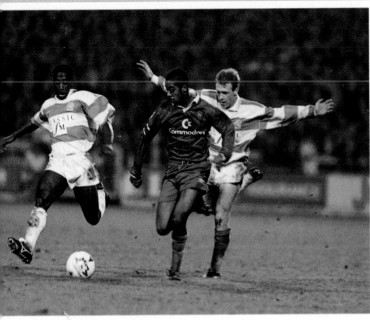

Left: Clive Wilson clears the ball, with colleague Simon Barker and Chelsea's Eddie Newton nearby.

READING

Elm Park, Norfolk Road, Reading, RG3 2EF

Tel No: 0734 507878
Advance Tickets Tel No: 0734 507878
League: 2nd Division
Brief History: Founded 1871. (Amalgamated with Reading Hornets in 1877 and with Earley in 1889). Former Grounds: Reading Recreation Ground, Reading Cricket Ground, Coley Park and Caversham Cricket Ground, moved to Elm Park in 1895. Founder-members Third Division (1920). Record attendance 33,042.
(Total) Current Capacity: 13,200 (2,100 Seated)

Visiting Supporters' Allocation: 3,081 (395 Seated)
Club Colours: White with blue hoops shirts, white shorts
Nearest Railway Station: Reading West
Parking (Car): Street parking
Parking (Coach/Bus): The Meadway
Police Force and Tel No: Thames Valley (0734 536000)
Disabled Visitors' Facilities
  Wheelchairs: Norfolk Road (few)
  Blind: No special facility

KEY

C Club Offices
S Club Shop
E Entrance(s) for visiting supporters
R Refreshment bars for visiting supporters
T Toilets for visiting supporters

⬆ North direction (approx)

❶ Tilehurst Road
❷ Norfolk Road
❸ County Cricket Ground
❹ Reading West BR Station (½ mile)
❺ Liebenrood Road to A4 Bath Road (¼ mile)

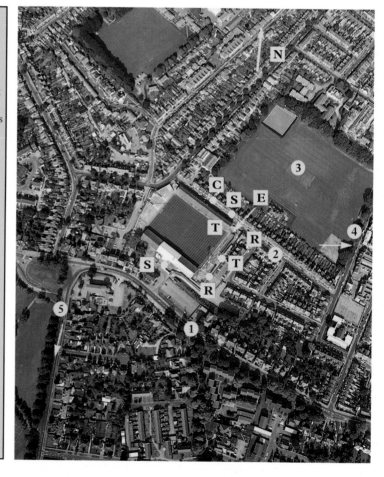

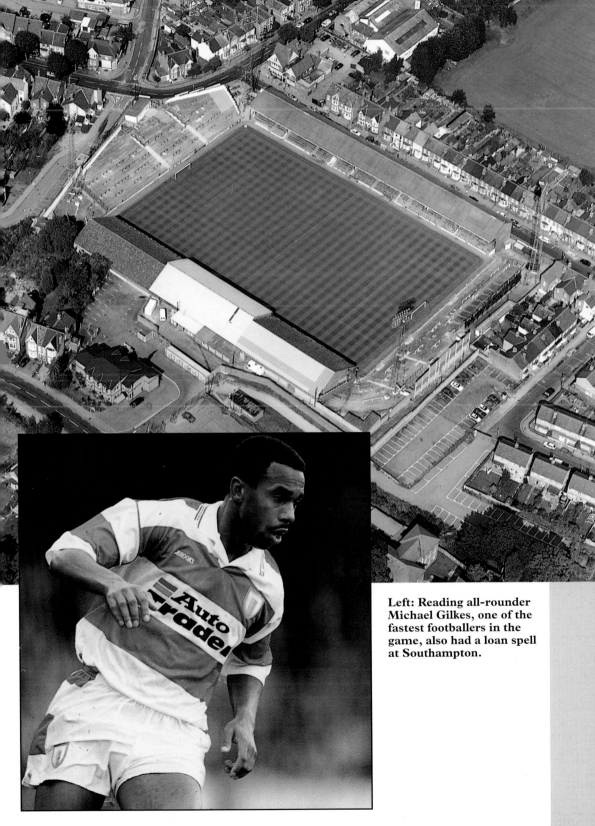

Left: Reading all-rounder Michael Gilkes, one of the fastest footballers in the game, also had a loan spell at Southampton.

ROCHDALE

Willbutts Lane, Spotland, Rochdale, OL11 5DS

Tel No: 0706 44648
Advance Tickets Tel No: 0706 44649
League: 3rd Division
Brief History: Founded 1907 from former
Rochdale Town F.C. (founded 1900).
Founder-members Third Division North
(1921). Record attendance 24,231.
(Total) Current Capacity: 10,735 (2,000
Seated)
Visiting Supporters' Allocation: 2,500 (none
Seated)
Club Colours: Blue & white shirts, blue & white
shorts

Nearest Railway Station: Rochdale
Parking (Car): Rear of ground
Parking (Coach/Bus): Rear of ground
Police Force and Tel No: Greater Manchester
(0706 47401)
Disabled Visitors' Facilities
  Wheelchairs: Main stand - disabled area
  Blind: No special facility
Anticipated Development(s): Childrens play
area planned

KEY

C Club Offices
S Club Shop
E Entrance(s) for visiting
  supporters
R Refreshment bars for visiting
  supporters
T Toilets for visiting supporters

↑ North direction (approx)

❶ Willbutts Lane
❷ A627 Edenfield Road
❸ Rochdale BR Station
  (½ mile)
❹ Sandy Lane

Left: Willbutts Lane favourite Jimmy Graham strikes a balletic pose in a February 93 encounter.

ROTHERHAM UNITED

Millmoor Ground, Rotherham, S60 1HR

Tel No: 0709 562434
Advance Tickets Tel No: 0709 562434
League: 2nd Division
Brief History: Founded 1877 (as Thornhill, later Thornhill United), changed name to Rotherham County in 1905 and to Rotherham United in 1925, (amalgamated with Rotherham Town - Football League members 1893-97 - in 1925). Former Grounds include: Red House Ground & Clifton Lane Cricket Ground, moved to Millmoor in 1907. Record attendance 25,000.
(Total) Current Capacity: 14,000 (3,407 Seated)

Visiting Supporters' Allocation: 4,000 (1,000 Seated)
Club Colours: Red shirts, white shorts
Nearest Railway Station: Rotherham Central
Parking (Car): Kimberworth and Main Street car parks, plus large car park adjacent to ground.
Parking (Coach/Bus): As directed by Police
Police Force and Tel No: South Yorkshire (0709 371121)
Disabled Visitors' Facilities
  Wheelchairs: Millmoor Lane
  Blind: No special facility

KEY

C Club Offices
S Club Shop
E Entrance(s) for visiting supporters
R Refreshment bars for visiting supporters
T Toilets for visiting supporters

↑ North direction (approx)

❶ Car Park
❷ Rotherham Central BR Station
❸ A6109 Masborough Road
❹ Millmoor Lane
❺ To A6178 and M1 Junction 34

Left: United's Shaun Goater winces after the impact from heading the ball, in a close contest with a Wigan player.

SCARBOROUGH

McCain Stadium, Seamer Road, Scarborough, N. Yorkshire YO12 4HF

Tel No: 0723 375094
Advance Tickets Tel No: 0723 375094
League: 3rd Division
Brief History: Founded 1879 as 'Scarborough Cricketers F.C.' changed name to 'Scarborough F.C.' in 1887. Former grounds: North Marine (Cricket) Ground and Recreation Ground, moved to (then named) Athletic Ground in 1898. Promoted to Football League in 1987. Record attendance 11,124.
(Total) Current Capacity: 8,177 (806 Seated)
Visiting Supporters' Allocation: 2,897 (288 Seated)

Club Colours: Red shirts, white shorts
Nearest Railway Station: Scarborough Central (2 miles)
Parking (Car): Street parking
Parking (Coach/Bus): Weaponess coach/car park
Police Force and Tel No: North Yorkshire (0723 363333)
Disabled Visitors' Facilities
  Wheelchairs: Main Stand, Edgehill Road end.
  Blind: No special facility

KEY

C Club Offices
S Club Shop
E Entrance(s) for visiting supporters
R Refreshment bars for visiting supporters
T Toilets for visiting supporters

↑ North direction (approx)

❶ A64 Seamer Road
❷ Scarborough Central BR Station (2 miles)
❸ To York
❹ McCain Stand

Left: Gary Himsworth outruns Arsenal defender David O'Leary in the Coca Cola League Cup match at the McCain Stadium.

SCUNTHORPE UNITED

Glanford Park, Doncaster Road, Scunthorpe DN15 8TD

Tel No: 0724 848077
Advance Tickets Tel No: 0724 848077
League: 3rd Division
Brief History: Founded 1899 as Scunthorpe United, amalgamated with North Lindsey to become 'Scunthorpe & Lindsey United in 1912. Changed name to Scunthorpe United in 1956. Former grounds: Crosby (Lindsey United) & Old Showground, moved to Glanford Park in 1988. Elected to Football League in 1950. Record attendance 8,775 (23,935 at Old Showground).

(Total) Current Capacity: 9,200 (6,400 Seated)
Club Colours: Sky blue shirts with two claret rings on sleeves, white shorts with claret stripe.
Nearest Railway Station: Scunthorpe
Parking (Car): At ground
Parking (Coach/Bus): At ground
Police Force and Tel No: Humberside (0724 282888)
Disabled Visitors' Facilities
  Wheelchairs: Clugston Stand
  Blind: Commentary available

KEY

C Club Offices
S Club Shop
E Entrance(s) for visiting supporters
R Refreshment bars for visiting supporters
T Toilets for visiting supporters

↑ North direction (approx)

❶ Car Park
❷ Glanford Stand
❸ A18 Doncaster Road
❹ Scunthorpe BR Station and Town Centre (1½ miles)
❺ M181 and M180 Junction 3

Left: United's Jason White shows a clean pair of heels to York's experienced Paul Stancliffe in the Glanford Park encounter.

SHEFFIELD UNITED

Bramall Lane, Sheffield, S2 4SU

Tel No: 0742 738955
Advance Tickets Tel No: 0742 766771
League: F.A. Premier
Brief History: Founded 1889. (Sheffield Wednesday occasionally used Bramall Lane c.1880). Founder-members 2nd Division (1892). Record attendance 68,287
(Total) Current Capacity: 30,845 (23,390 Seated)
Visiting Supporters' Allocation: 7,160 (2,560 Seated)

Club Colours: Red & white striped shirts, black shorts
Nearest Railway Station: Sheffield Midland
Parking (Car): Street parking
Parking (Coach/Bus): As directed by Police
Police Force and Tel No: South Yorkshire (0472 768522)
Disabled Visitors' Facilities
  Wheelchairs: Westfield Health Enclosure (John Street)
  Blind: Commentary available

KEY
C Club Offices
E Entrance(s) for visiting supporters
R Refreshment bars for visiting supporters
T Toilets for visiting supporters

↑ North direction (approx)

❶ A621 Bramall Lane
❷ Shoreham Street
❸ Car Park
❹ Sheffield Midland BR Station (1/4 mile)
❺ John Street
❻ Spion Kop

Left: Brian Deane, the Blades' striker - partly hidden by Gary Pallister of Manchester United - scores to put the home team in front.

SHEFFIELD WEDNESDAY

Hillsborough, Sheffield, S6 1SW

Tel No: 0742 343122
Advance Tickets Tel No: 0742 337233
League: F.A. Premier
Brief History: Founded 1867 as The Wednesday F.C. (changed to Sheffield Wednesday c.1930). Former Grounds: London Road, Wyrtle Road (Heeley), Sheaf House Ground, Encliffe & Olive Grove (Bramall Lane also used occasionally), moved to Hillsborough (then named 'Owlerton' in 1899). Founder-members Second Division (1892). Record attendance 72,841.
(Total) Current Capacity: 41,237 (23,370 Seated)

Visiting Supporters' Allocation: 4,183 (4,183 Seated)
Club Colours: Blue & white striped shirts, black shorts
Nearest Railway Station: Sheffield (4 miles)
Parking (Car): Street Parking
Parking (Coach/Bus): Owlerton Stadium
Police Force and Tel No: South Yorkshire (0742 343131)
Disabled Visitors' Facilities
  Wheelchairs: North Stand
  Blind: Commentary available

KEY

C Club Offices
S Club Shop
E Entrance(s) for visiting supporters

↑ North direction (approx)

❶ Leppings Lane
❷ River Dom
❸ A61 Penistone Road North
❹ Sheffield BR Station and City Centre (4 miles)
❺ Spion Kop
❻ To M1 (North)
❼ To M1 (South)

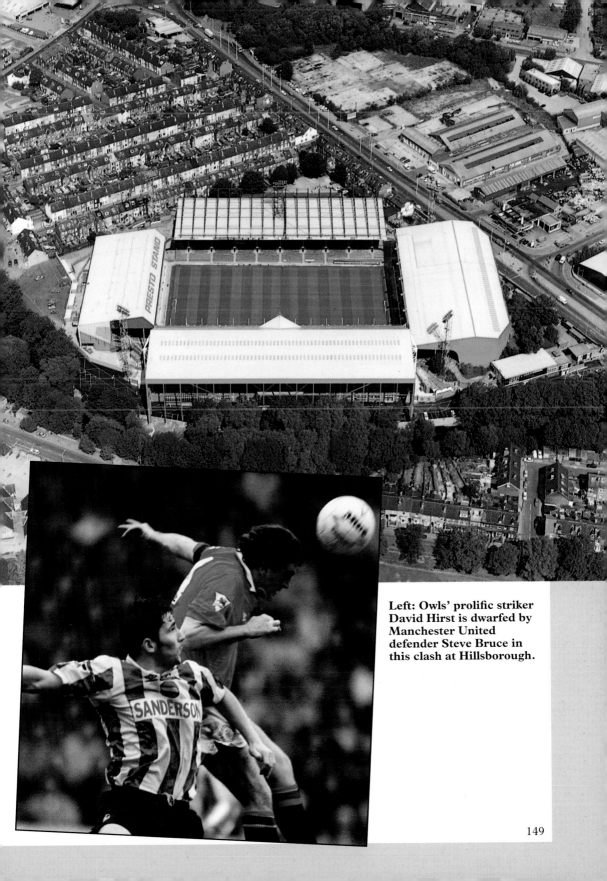

Left: Owls' prolific striker David Hirst is dwarfed by Manchester United defender Steve Bruce in this clash at Hillsborough.

SHREWSBURY TOWN

Gay Meadow, Shrewsbury, SY2 6AB

Tel No: 0743 360111
Advance Tickets Tel No: 0743 360111
League: 3rd Division
Brief History: Founded 1886. Former Grounds: Monkmoor Racecourse, Ambler's Field & The Barracks Ground (moved to Gay Meadow in 1910). Elected to Football League in 1950. Record attendance 18,917
(Total) Current Capacity: 15,000 (4,500 Seated)
Club Colours: Blue, Yellow & white shirts and shorts

Nearest Railway Station: Shrewsbury
Parking (Car): Adjacent car park
Parking (Coach/Bus): Gay Meadow
Police Force and Tel No: West Mercia (0743 232888)
Disabled Visitors' Facilities
  Wheelchairs: Alongside Pitch (as directed)
  Blind: No special facility
Anticipated Development(s): Negotiations to re-locate Ground in 1995.

KEY
- **C** Club Offices
- **S** Club Shop
- **E** Entrance(s) for visiting supporters
- **R** Refreshment bars for visiting supporters
- **T** Toilets for visiting supporters

↑ North direction (approx)

- ❶ Entrance road to ground
- ❷ Wyle Cup
- ❸ River Severn
- ❹ Car Parks
- ❺ Shrewsbury BR Station (1 mile — shortest route)
- ❻ Riverside enclosure

Right: The Shrews' Howard Clarke is beaten to the ball by former Sunderland defender Nick Pickering of Darlington.

SOUTHAMPTON

The Dell, Milton Road, Southampton, SO9 4XX

Tel No: 0703 220505
Advance Tickets Tel No: 0703 228575
League: F.A. Premier
Brief History: Founded 1885 as 'Southampton St. Mary's Young Mens Association' (changed name to Southampton in 1897). Former Grounds: Northlands Road, Antelope Ground, County Ground, moved to The Dell in 1898. Founder-members Third Division (1920). Record attendance 31,044.
(Total) Current Capacity: 21,909 (8,808 Seated)
Visiting Supporters' Allocation: 2,438 (526 Seated)
Club Colours: Red & white shirts, black shorts

Nearest Railway Station: Southampton
Parking (Car): Street parking
Parking (Coach/Bus): As directed by Police
Police Force and Tel No: Hampshire (0703 581111)
Disabled Visitors' Facilities
Wheelchairs: Milton Road (book in advance)
Blind: Commentary available (book in advance)
Anticipated Development(s): Redevelopment of both ends of Ground, Summer 1993. Conversion to full seating on two sides, Summer 1994. Redevelopment of West Stand in 1996 or long term re-location plan.

KEY
- **C** Club Offices
- **S** Club Shop
- **E** Entrance(s) for visiting supporters
- **R** Refreshment bars for visiting supporters
- **T** Toilets for visiting supporters

↑ North direction (approx)

❶ Archers Road
❷ Milton Road
❸ Southampton BR Station
❹ Hill Lane

**Right: The Saints'
Northern Ireland striker
Iain Dowie in typically
forceful action, leaving the
Manchester City player
behind.**

SOUTHEND UNITED

Roots Hall Ground, Victoria Avenue, Southend-on-Sea, SS2 6NQ

Tel No: 0702 340707
Advance Tickets Tel No: 0702 435602
League: 1st Division
Brief History: Founded 1906. Former Grounds: Roots Hall, Kursaal, The Stadium Grainger Road, moved to Roots Hall (new Ground) 1955. Founder-members Third Division (1920). Record attendance 31,033.
(Total) Current Capacity: 13,598 (6,124 Seated)

Club Colours: Blue with yellow trim shirts, yellow shorts
Nearest Railway Station: Prittlewell
Parking (Car): Street parking
Parking (Coach/Bus): Car park at Ground
Police Force and Tel No: Essex (0702 431212)
Disabled Visitors' Facilities
   Wheelchairs: West Stand
   Blind: Commentary available

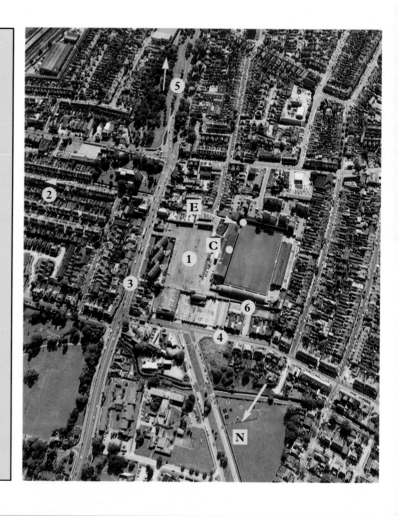

KEY
C Club Offices
E Entrance(s) for visiting supporters

↑ North direction (approx)

❶ Car Park
❷ Prittlewell BR Station (¼ mile)
❸ A127 Victoria Avenue
❹ Fairfax Drive
❺ Southend centre (½ mile)
❻ North Bank

Right: At £165,000, possibly the buy of the season - Stan Collymore in action at Roots Hall.

155

STOCKPORT COUNTY

Edgeley Park, Hardcastle Road, Edgeley, Stockport, SK3 9DD

Tel No: 061 480 8888
Advance Tickets Tel No: 061 480 8888
League: 2nd Division
Brief History: Founded 1883 as Heaton Norris Rovers, changed name to Stockport County in 1890. Former Grounds: Heaton Norris Recreation Ground, Heaton Norris Wanderers Cricket Ground, Chorlton's Farm, Ash Inn Ground, Wilkes Field (Belmont Street) and Nursery Inn (Green Lane), moved to Edgeley Park in 1902. Record attendance 27,833.
(Total) Current Capacity: 8,500 (1,800 Seated)

Club Colours: Blue shirts with red & white flashes, white shorts
Nearest Railway Station: Stockport
Parking (Car): Street parking
Parking (Coach/Bus): As directed by Police
Police Force and Tel No: Greater Manchester (061 872 5050)
Disabled Visitors' Facilities
  Wheelchairs: Main Stand
  Blind: No special facility

KEY

C Club Offices
E Entrance(s) for visiting supporters
R Refreshment bars for visiting supporters
T Toilets for visiting supporters

↑ North direction (approx)

❶ Mercian Way
❷ Hardcastle Road
❸ Stockport BR Station (¼ mile)
❹ Railway End
❺ Main Stand

156

Left: County's Peter Ward gets in a timely tackle on Port Vale's stalwart Ray Walker in the 2nd Division clash at Vale Park.

STOKE CITY

Victoria Ground, Boothen Old Road, Stoke-on-Trent, ST4 4EG

Tel No: 0782 413511
Advance Tickets Tel No: 0782 413961
League: 1st Division
Brief History: Founded 1863 as Stoke F.C., amalgamated with Stoke Victoria in 1878, changed to Stoke City in 1925. Former Ground: Sweetings Field, moved to Victoria Ground in 1878. Founder-members Football League (1888). Record attendance 51,380.
(Total) Current Capacity: 25,084 (9,625 Seated)

Club Colours: Red & white striped shirts, white shorts
Nearest Railway Station: Stoke-on-Trent
Parking (Car): Car park at ground
Parking (Coach/Bus): Whieldon Road
Police Force and Tel No: Staffordshire (0784 744644)
Disabled Visitors' Facilities
　Wheelchairs: Corner Butler Street/Boothen End
　Blind: Limited facilities (contact first)

KEY
C Club Offices
S Club Shop
E Entrance(s) for visiting supporters

↑ North direction (approx)

❶ Car Park
❷ Campbell Road
❸ A500 Queensway
❹ M6 Junction 15 (4 miles via A500)
❺ Stoke-on-Trent BR Station (1/2 mile)

Left: Stoke's John Butler, and Exeter's Andy Harris become entangled when they challenge for the ball at the Victoria Ground.

SUNDERLAND

Roker Park, Grantham Road, Roker, Sunderland, SR6 9SW

Tel No: 091 514 0332
Advance Tickets Tel No: 091 514 0332
League: 1st Division
Brief History: Founded 1879 as 'Sunderland and District Teachers Association', changed to 'Sunderland Association' (in 1880) and shortly after to 'Sunderland'. Former Grounds: Blue House Field, Groves Field (Ashbrooke), Horatio Street, Abbs Field & Newcastle Road, moved to Roker Park in 1898. Record attendance 75,118
(Total) Current Capacity: 31,222 (7,753 Seated)

Club Colours: Red & white striped shirts, black shorts
Nearest Railway Station: Seaburn
Parking (Car): Car park adjacent ground
Parking (Coach/Bus): Seafront, Roker
Police Force and Tel No: Northumbria (091 567 6155)
Disabled Visitors' Facilities
   Wheelchairs: Roker Baths Road
   Blind: Commentary available
Anticipated Development(s): Possible move to new 48,000 all-seater Stadium, 1995/96 season.

KEY
- **C** Club Offices
- **S** Club Shop
- **E** Entrance(s) for visiting supporters

↑ North direction (approx)

❶ Roker Baths Road
❷ Grantham Road
❸ Seaburn BR Station (1 mile)
❹ To A1018 Newcastle Road
❺ Hampden Road
❻ To A183 Roker Terrace (Seafront)
❼ Car Park

Left: Sunderland's stylish defender Gary Bennett in a close encounter with Jon Goodman of Millwall.

SWANSEA CITY

Vetch Field, Swansea, SA1 3SU

Tel No: 0792 474114
Advance Tickets Tel No: 0792 474114
League: 2nd Division
Brief History: Founded 1900 as Swansea Town, changed to Swansea City in 1970. Former Grounds: various, including Recreation Ground. Moved to Vetch Field in 1912. Founder-members Third Division (1920). Record attendance 32,796.
(Total) Current Capacity: 16,419 (3,414 Seated)
Club Colours: White shirts, white shorts

Nearest Railway Station: Swansea High Street
Parking (Car): Kingsway car park & adjacent Clarence Terrace, (supervised car park).
Parking (Coach/Bus): As directed by Police
Police Force and Tel No: South Wales (0792 456999)
Disabled Visitors' Facilities
  Wheelchairs: Glamorgan Street
  Blind: No special facility
Anticipated Development(s): New 6,500 seated Stand on North Bank and new dressing rooms, community hall and offices.

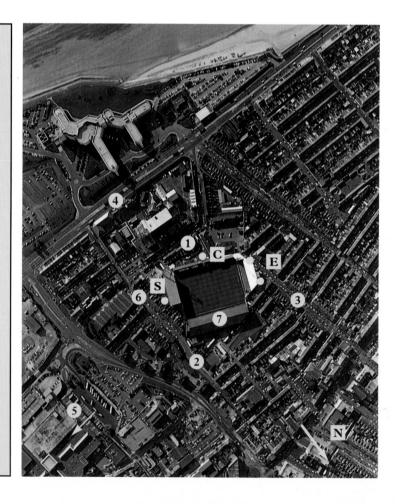

KEY
- **C** Club Offices
- **S** Club Shop
- **E** Entrance(s) for visiting supporters

↑ North direction (approx)

1. Glamorgan Street
2. William Street
3. Richardson Street
4. A4067 Oystermouth Road (8 miles to M4 Junction 42)
5. Swansea High Street BR Station (½ mile)
6. Supervised Car Park
7. North Bank

Right: Much travelled and much admired Colin West pictured in the Swansea City change strip.

SWINDON TOWN

County Ground, County Road, Swindon, SN1 2ED

Tel No: 0793 430430
Advance Tickets Tel No: 0793 430430
League: F. A. Premier
Brief History: Founded 1881. Former Grounds: Quarry Ground, Globe Field, Croft Ground, County Ground (adjacent to current ground and now Cricket Ground), moved to current County Ground in 1896. Founder-members Third Division (1920). Record attendance 32,000
(Total) Current Capacity: 18,158 (9,221 Seated)

Visiting Supporters' Allocation: 3,500 (200 Seated)
Club Colours: Red shirts, red shorts
Nearest Railway Station: Swindon
Parking (Car): Adjacent car park
Parking (Coach/Bus): Adjacent car park
Police Force and Tel No: Wiltshire (0793 528111)
Disabled Visitors' Facilities
  Wheelchairs: Town End Stand
  Blind: Commentary available

KEY

C Club Offices
S Club Shop
E Entrance(s) for visiting supporters
R Refreshment bars for visiting supporters
T Toilets for visiting supporters

↑ North direction (approx)

❶ Shrivenham Road
❷ County Road
❸ A345 Queens Drive (M4 Junction 15 – 3¹/₂ miles)
❹ Swindon BR Station (¹/₂ mile)
❺ Town End
❻ Car Park
❼ County Cricket Ground

Right: It's neck and neck as Swindon's Australian international Dave Mitchell clashes with Chris Burns of Portsmouth.

TORQUAY UNITED

Plainmoor Ground, Torquay TQ1 3PS

Telephone: 0803 328666
Advance Tickets Telephone: 0803 328666
League: 3rd Division
Brief History: Founded 1898, as Torquay United, amalgamated with Ellacombe in 1910, changed name to Torquay Town. Amalgamated with Babbacombe in 1921, changed name to Torquay United. Former grounds: Teignmouth Road, Torquay Recreation Ground, Cricketfield Road & Torquay Cricket Ground, moved to Plainmoor (Ellacombe Ground) in 1910. Record attendance 21,908.
Total Current Capacity: 6,455 (2,324 Seated)
Visiting Supporters Allocation: 1,248 (200 Seated)

Club Colours: Yellow with white stripe shirts, navy shorts

Nearest Railway Station: Torquay (2 miles)

Parking (Car): Street parking

Parking (Coach/Bus): Lymington Road coach station

Police Force and Tel. No.: Devon & Cornwall (0803 214491)

Disabled Visitors Facilities:
Wheelchairs: Homelands Lane
Blind: Commentary available

KEY
C Club Offices
S Club Shop
E Entrance(s) for visiting supporters
R Refreshment bars for visiting supporters
T Toilets for visiting supporters

⬆ North direction (approx)

❶ Warbro Road
❷ B3202 Marychurch Road
❸ Marnham Road
❹ Torquay BR Station (2 miles)

Left: Justin Fashanu in action for Torquay in February 93.

TOTTENHAM HOTSPUR

White Hart Lane, 748 High Road, Tottenham, London N17 0AP

Tel No: 081 808 6666
Advance Tickets Tel No: 081 808 8080
League: F. A. Premier
Brief History: Founded 1882 as 'Hotspur', changed name to Tottenham Hotspur in 1885. Former Grounds: Tottenham Marshes and Northumberland Park, moved to White Hart Lane in 1899. F. A. Cup winner 1901 (as a non-League club). Record attendance 75,038
(Total) Current Capacity: 33,740 (25,883 Seated)
Visiting Supporters' Allocation: 2,481 (2,481 Seated – maximum)
Club Colours: White shirts, navy blue shorts

Nearest Railway Station: White Hart Lane plus Seven Sisters & Manor House (tube)
Parking (Car): Street parking (min $\frac{1}{4}$ mile from ground)
Parking (Coach/Bus): Northumberland Park coach park
Police Force and Tel No: Metropolitan (081 801 3443)
Disabled Visitors' Facilities
 Wheelchairs: Paxton Road and High Road (by prior arrangement)
 Blind: No special facility
Anticipated Development(s): Conversion to all-seater Ground by August 1994

KEY

C Club Offices
S Club Shop
E Entrance(s) for visiting supporters
R Refreshment bars for visiting supporters
T Toilets for visiting supporters

⬆ North direction (approx)

❶ Park Lane
❷ A1010 High Road
❸ White Hart Lane BR Station
❹ Paxton Road
❺ Worcester Avenue
❻ West Stand

Left: John Fashanu of Wimbledon fights for a high ball with Spurs' Neil Ruddock in this London derby match.

TRANMERE ROVERS

Prenton Park, Prenton Road West, Birkenhead, L42 9PN

Tel No: 051 608 3677
Advance Tickets Tel No: 051 608 3677
League: 1st Division
Brief History: Founded 1884 as Belmont F.C., changed name to Tranmere Rovers in 1885 (not connected to earlier 'Tranmere Rovers'). Former grounds: Steele's Field and Ravenshaw's Field (also known as Old Prenton Park, ground of Tranmere Rugby Club), moved to (new) Prenton Park in 1911. Founder-members 3rd Division North (1921). Record attendance 24,424.
(Total) Current Capacity: 17,452 (3,800 Seated)

Visiting Supporters' Allocation: 3,960 (368 Seated)
Club Colours: White shirts, white shorts
Nearest Railway Station: Hamilton Square or Rock Ferry
Parking (Car): Car park at Ground
Parking (Coach/Bus): Car park at Ground
Police Force and Tel No: Merseyside (051 709 6010)
Disabled Visitors' Facilities
 Wheelchairs: Main Stand
 Blind: No special facility

KEY

C Club Offices
S Club Shop
E Entrance(s) for visiting supporters
R Refreshment bars for visiting supporters
T Toilets for visiting supporters

⬆ North direction (approx)

❶ Car Park
❷ Prenton Road West
❸ Borough Road
❹ M53 Junction 4 (B5151) – 3 miles
❺ Birkenhead (1 mile)

Right: Welshman John Aldridge - who started in the League with now defunct Newport County - a prolific goalscorer for Rovers.

WALSALL

Bescot Stadium, Bescot Crescent, Walsall, West Midlands, WS1 4SA

Tel No: 0922 22791
Advance Tickets Tel No: 0922 22791
League: 3rd Division
Brief History: Founded 1888 as Walsall Town Swifts (amalgamation of Walsall Town - founded 1884 - and Walsall Swifts - founded 1885), changed name to Walsall in 1895. Former Grounds: The Chuckery, West Bromwich Road (twice), Hilary Street (later named Fellows Park, twice), moved to Bescot Stadium in 1990. Founder-members Second Division (1892). Record attendance 10,628 (24,100 at Fellows Park).

(Total) Current Capacity: 9,485 (6,685 Seated)
Visiting Supporters' Allocation: 1,916 (1,916 Seated)
Club Colours: Red shirts, red shorts
Nearest Railway Station: Bescot
Parking (Car): Car park at Ground
Parking (Coach/Bus): Car park at Ground
Police Force and Tel No : West Midlands (0922 38111)
Disabled Visitors' Facilities
  Wheelchairs: Highgate Stand
  Blind: Commentary planned

KEY

C Club Offices
S Club Shop
E Entrance(s) for visiting supporters
R Refreshment bars for visiting supporters
T Toilets for visiting supporters

↑ North direction (approx)

❶ Motorway M6
❷ M6 Junction 9
❸ Bescot BR Station
❹ Car Parks
❺ Bescot Crescent

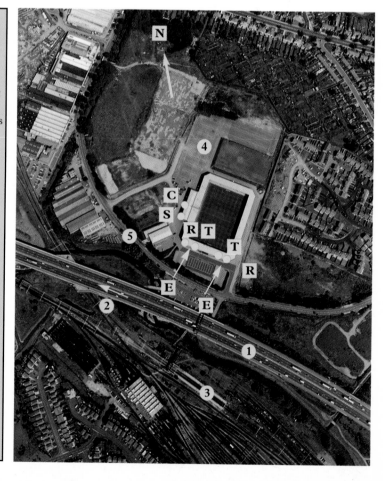

Left: Wayne Clarke (in red) in close contact with a Scarborough player during the 3rd Division match at Bescot Stadium.

WATFORD

Vicarage Road Stadium, Watford, WD1 8ER

Tel No: 0923 230933
Advance Tickets Tel No: 0923 220393
League: 1st Division
Brief History: Founded 1898 as an amalgamation of West Herts (founded 1891) and Watford St. Mary's (founded early 1890s). Former Grounds: Wiggenhall Road (Watford St. Mary's) and West Herts Sports Ground, moved to Vicarage Road in 1922. Founder-members Third Division (1920). Record attendance 34,099.
(Total) Current Capacity: 23,596 (6,906 Seated)
Club Colours: Yellow with black & red shirts, red with yellow & black shorts.

Nearest Railway Station: Watford West (major games) and/or Watford High Street
Parking (Car): Nearby multi-storey car park in town centre (10 mins walk)
Parking (Coach/Bus): Cardiff Road car park
Police Force and Tel No: Hertfordshire (0923 244444)
Disabled Visitors' Facilities
  Wheelchairs: Corner East Stand and South Terrace (special enclosure for approx. 20 wheelchairs)
  Blind: Commentary available

KEY
C Club Offices
S Club Shop
E Entrance(s) for visiting supporters
R Refreshment bars for visiting supporters

↑ North direction (approx)

❶ Vicarage Road
❷ Occupation Road
❸ Rous Stand
❹ Town Centre (½ mile) – Car Parks, High Street BR Station
❺ Watford West BR Station

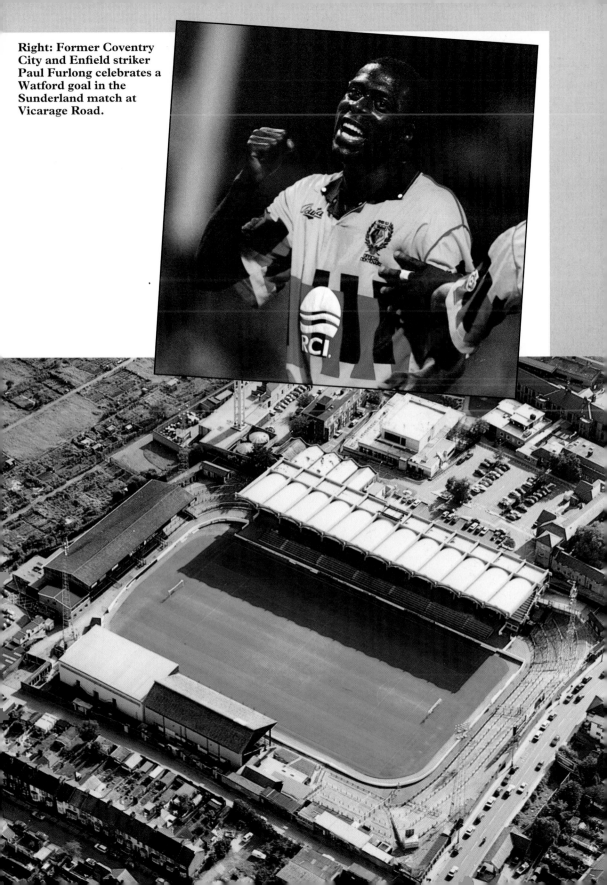

Right: Former Coventry City and Enfield striker Paul Furlong celebrates a Watford goal in the Sunderland match at Vicarage Road.

WEST BROMWICH ALBION

The Hawthorns, Halfords Lane, West Bromwich, West Midlands, B71 4LF

Tel No: 021 525 8888

Advance Tickets Tel No: 021 553 5472

League: 1st Division

Brief History: Founded 1879. Former Grounds: Coopers Hill, Dartmouth Park, Four Acres, Stoney Lane, moved to the Hawthorns in 1900. Founder-members of Football League (1888). Record attendance 64,815.

(Total) Current Capacity: 33,781 (10,397 Seated)

Club Colours: Navy blue & white striped shirts, white shorts

Nearest Railway Station: Rolfe Street, Smethwick (1$\frac{1}{2}$ miles)

Parking (Car): Halfords Lane & Rainbow Stand car parks.

Parking (Coach/Bus): Rainbow Stand car park

Police Force and Tel No: West Midlands (021 554 3414)

Disabled Visitors' Facilities
   Wheelchairs: Corner Birmingham Road/Main Stand
   Blind: Facility available

Anticipated Development(s): Re-development of Smethwick End.

KEY

- **C** Club Offices
- **S** Club Shop
- **E** Entrance(s) for visiting supporters
- **T** Toilets for visiting supporters

↑ North direction (approx)

❶ A41 Birmingham Road
❷ M5 Junction 1 (³/4 mile)
❸ Birmingham centre (4 miles)
❹ Halfords Lane
❺ Main Stand
❻ Smethwick End
❼ Rolfe Street, Smethwick BR Station (1¹/2 miles)

Left: 'Keeper Stuart Naylor punches clear during the home match with 2nd division table-topping Stoke City.

WEST HAM UNITED

Boleyn Ground, Green Street, Upton Park, London, E13 9AZ

Tel No: 081 472 2740
Advance Tickets Tel No: 081 472 3322
League: F. A. Premier
Brief History: Founded 1895 as Thames Ironworks, changed name to West Ham United in 1900. Former Grounds: Hermit Road, Browning Road, The Memorial Ground, moved to Boleyn Ground in 1904. Record attendance 42,322.
(Total) Current Capacity: 22,503 (11,600 Seated)
Visiting Supporters' Allocation: 3,000 (500 Seated)
Club Colours: Claret & blue shirts, white shorts.

Nearest Railway Station: Barking BR, Upton Park (tube)
Parking (Car): Street parking
Parking (Coach/Bus): As directed by police
Police Force and Tel No: Metropolitan (081 593 8232)
Disabled Visitors' Facilities
　Wheelchairs: Green Street
　Blind: No special facility
Anticipated Development(s): Re-development of North and South Bank Terraces and East Terrace, to convert to all-seater stadium, by August 1994.

KEY

C Club Offices
S Club Shop
E Entrance(s) for visiting supporters
R Refreshment bars for visiting supporters
T Toilets for visiting supporters

↑ North direction (approx)

❶ A124 Barking Road
❷ Green Street
❸ North Bank
❹ Upton Park Tube Station (¼ mile)
❺ Barking BR Station (1 mile)

Right: At Molineux, Hammers' Clive Allen gets to the ball first, beating Wolverhampton's Paul Cook.

WIGAN ATHLETIC

Springfield Park, Wigan, Lancs, WN6 7BA

Tel No: 0942 44433
Advance Tickets Tel No: 0942 44433
League: 3rd Division
Brief History: Founded 1932. Springfield Park used by former club Wigan Borough (Football League 1921-31) but unrelated to current club. Elected to Football League in 1978 (the last club to be elected rather than promoted). Record attendance 27,500.
(Total) Current Capacity: 9,895 (1,272 Seated)
Visiting Supporters' Allocation: 2,000 (311 Seated)

Club Colours: Blue shirts, blue with white & red trim shorts
Nearest Railway Station: Wallgate and North Western (1 mile)
Parking (Car): Street parking
Parking (Coach/Bus): At Ground
Police Force and Tel No: Greater Manchester (0942 44981)
Disabled Visitors' Facilities
   Wheelchairs: Phoenix Stand side
   Blind: Commentary available

KEY
C Club Offices
S Club Shop
E Entrance(s) for visiting supporters
R Refreshment bars for visiting supporters
T Toilets for visiting supporters

↑ North direction (approx)

❶ Car Park
❷ Springfield Road
❸ St. Andrews Drive
❹ Wallgate and North Western BR Stations (1 mile)
❺ B5375 Woodhouse Lane

Left: Gary Powell of Wigan jumps high, as two Rotherham players look on, during the 2nd Division match at Springfield Park.

WIMBLEDON

Selhurst Park, London, SE25 6PU

Tel No: 081 771 2233
Advance Tickets Tel No: 081 771 8841
League: F.A. Premier
Brief History: Founded 1889 as Wimbledon Old Centrals, changed name to Wimbledon in 1905. Former Grounds: Wimbledon Common, Pepy's Road, Grand Drive, Merton Hall Road, Malden Wanderers Cricket Ground & Plough Lane. Moved to Selhurst Park (Crystal Palace F.C. Ground) in 1991. Elected to Football League in 1977. Record attendance (Plough Lane) 18,000.
(Total) Current Capacity: 30,115 (15,515 Seated)

Visiting Supporters' Allocation: 5,537 (2,337 Seated)
Club Colours: Blue shirts, blue shorts
Nearest Railway Station: Selhurst, Norwood Junction & Thornton Heath
Parking (Car): Street parking & Sainsbury's car park
Parking (Coach/Bus): Thornton Heath
Police Force and Tel No: Metropolitan (081 653 8568)
Disabled Visitors' Facilities
  Wheelchairs: Park Road Stand (limited)
  Blind: Commentary available

KEY
C Club Offices
S Club Shop
E Entrance(s) for visiting supporters
R Refreshment bars for visiting supporters
T Toilets for visiting supporters

↑ North direction (approx)

❶ Whitehorse Lane
❷ Park Road
❸ A213 Selhurst Road
❹ Selhurst BR Station (1/2 mile)
❺ Norwood Junction BR Station
❻ Thornton Heath BR Station (1/2 mile)
❼ Car Park (Sainsbury's)

Right: John Fashanu and Manchester City's Michael Vonk, are both determined to win the ball during this Premier League match.

WOLVERHAMPTON WANDERERS

Molineux Ground, Waterloo Road, Wolverhampton, WV1 4QR

Tel No: 0902 712181
Advance Tickets Tel No: 0902 25899
League: 1st Division
Brief History: Founded 1877 as St. Lukes, combined with Goldthorn Hill to become Wolverhampton Wanderers in 1884. Former Grounds: Old Windmill Field, John Harper's Field and Dudley Road, moved to Molineux in 1889. Founder-members Football League (1888). Record attendance 61,315
(Total) Current Capacity: 19,300 (14,300 Seated)

Club Colours: Gold shirts, black shorts
Nearest Railway Station: Wolverhampton
Parking (Car): West Park and adjacent North Bank
Parking (Coach/Bus): As directed by Police
Police Force and Tel No: West Midlands (0902 27851)
Disabled Visitors' Facilities
  Wheelchairs: North Bank
  Blind: Commentary (by prior arrangement).
Anticipated Development(s): New South Bank Stand completion by December 1993.

KEY
C Club Offices
S Club Shop
E Entrance(s) for visiting supporters
R Refreshment bars for visiting supporters
T Toilets for visiting supporters

↑ North direction (approx)

❶ Stan Cullis Stand
❷ John Ireland Stand
❸ Billy Wright Stand
❹ Ring Road – St. Peters
❺ Waterloo Road
❻ A449 Stafford Street
❼ BR Station (1/2 mile)

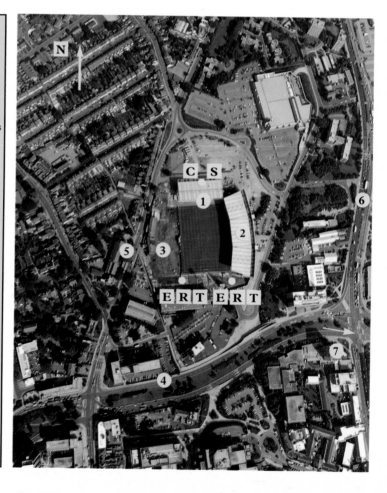

Left: England international Steve Bull in action in the 1st Division match with Derby County.

WREXHAM

Racecourse Ground, Mold Road, Wrexham, Clwyd LL11 2AN

Tel No: 0978 262129
Advance Tickets Tel No: 0978 262129
League: 2nd Division
Brief History: Founded 1873 (oldest Football Club in Wales). Former Ground: Acton Park, permanent move to Racecourse Ground c.1900. Founder-members Third Division North (1921). Record attendance 34,445.
(Total) Current Capacity: 17,500 (5,026 Seated)
Visiting Supporters' Allocation: 4,130 (2,230 Seated)

Club Colours: Red shirts, white shorts
Nearest Railway Station: Wrexham General
Parking (Car): (Nearby) Town car parks
Parking (Coach/Bus): As directed by Police
Police Force and Tel No: Wrexham Division (0978 290222)

Disabled Visitors' Facilities
  Wheelchairs: Mold Road Side
  Blind: Commentary available

KEY

C Club Offices
S Club Shop
E Entrance(s) for visiting supporters
R Refreshment bars for visiting supporters
T Toilets for visiting supporters

↑ North direction (approx)

❶ Wrexham General BR Station
❷ A541 – Mold Road
❸ Wrexham Town Centre
❹ Car Park
❺ Kop Town End

Right: Wrexham's Micky Thomas scrambles to recover, together with Mark Barham of Shrewsbury.

WYCOMBE WANDERERS

Adams Park, Hillbottom Road, Sands, High Wycombe, Bucks, HP12 4HU.

Tel No: 0494 472100
Advance Tickets Tel No: 0494 472100
League: 3rd Division
Brief History: Founded 1884. Former Grounds: The Rye, Spring Meadows, Loakes Park, moved to Adams Park 1990. Promoted to Football League 1993. Record attendance 15,678 (Loakes Park)
(Total) Current Capacity: 7,200 (1,267 Seated)
Visiting Supporters' Allocation: 500 (Seated 90 min.)

Club Colours: Cambridge and Oxford blue quartered shirts, blue shorts.
Nearest Railway Station: High Wycombe (2 1/2 miles)
Parking (Car): At Ground and Street parking
Parking (Coach/Bus): At Ground
Police Force and Tel No: Thames Valley 0296 396534
Disabled Visitors' Facilities
   Wheelchairs: Special shelter - Main Stand, Hillbottom Road end
   Blind: Commentary available

KEY
C Club Offices
S Club Shop
E Entrance(s) for visiting supporters
R Refreshment bars for visiting supporters
T Toilets for visiting supporters

↑ North direction (approx)

❶ Car Park
❷ Hillbottom Road (Industrial Estate)
❸ M40 Junction 4 (approx. 2 miles)
❹ Wycombe Town Centre (approx. 2 1/2 miles)

Left: Simon Hutchinson (in blue) of Wycombe Wanderers helps the team towards the GM Vauxhall Conference title.

YORK CITY

Bootham Crescent, York, YO3 7AQ

Tel No: 0904 624447
Advance Tickets Tel No: 0904 624447
League: 2nd Division
Brief History: Founded 1922. Former ground: Fulfordgate Ground, moved to Bootham Crescent in 1932. Record attendance 28,123.
(Total) Current Capacity: 12,475 (3,245 Seated)
Visiting Supporters' Allocation: 4,456 (336 Seated)

Club Colours: Red shirts, blue shorts
Nearest Railway Station: York
Parking (Car): Street parking
Parking (Coach/Bus): As directed by Police
Police Force and Tel No: North Yorkshire (0904 631321)
Disabled Visitors' Facilities
   Wheelchairs: In front of Family Stand
   Blind: Commentary available

KEY

C Club Offices
S Club Shop
E Entrance(s) for visiting supporters
R Refreshment bars for visiting supporters
T Toilets for visiting supporters

↑ North direction (approx)

❶ Bootham Crescent
❷ Grosvenor Road
❸ Burton Stone Lane
❹ York BR Station (1 mile)

Right: City's Nigel Pepper is in full control during the home match with Doncaster.

Aerofilms Limited

Aerofilms was founded in 1919 and has specialised in the acquisition of aerial photography within the United Kingdom throughout its history. The company has a record of being innovative in the uses and applications of aerial photography.

Photographs looking at the environment in perspective are called oblique aerial photographs. These are taken with Hasselblad cameras by professional photographers experienced in the difficult conditions encountered in aerial work.

Photographs looking straight down at the landscape are termed vertical aerial photographs. These photographs are obtained using Leica survey cameras, the products from which are normally used in the making of maps.

Aerofilms has a unique library of oblique and vertical photographs in excess of one and a half million in number covering the United Kingdom. This library of photographs dates from 1919 to the present and is continually being updated.

Oblique and vertical photography can be taken to customers' specification by Aerofilms' professional photographers. Completely new photography has been taken of all the grounds featured in this book.

To discover more of the wealth of past or present photographs held in the library at Aerofilms or to commission new aerial photography to your requirements, please contact:

Aerofilms Limited
Gate Studios
Station Road
Borehamwood
Herts WD6 1EJ

Telephone 081-207-0666
Fax 081-207-5433

Readers who wish to purchase copies of any of the oblique aerial photographs featured in this book are referred to the order form which appears on another page.